The Famous Five and You
Run Away!

3

Join the Famous Five on their intrepid
adventure on Kirrin Island. Signals from a
boat at sea could mean smugglers at work,
but then the Five hear a child scream. *You*
can choose how the Five rescue the girl –
but will you be too late?

This exciting game story is based on Enid
Blyton's *Five Run Away Together*.

Join the action in
The Famous Five and You!

Enid Blyton, who died in 1968 at the age of 71 became, during her lifetime, Britain's best-loved and most popular author, and is still considered to have wielded a greater influence than any other author over children's writing in the post-war years. She loved young people, and wrote for 'all children, any children, everywhere' – over 600 books, many songs, poems and plays.

THE FAMOUS FIVE & YOU ③

RUN AWAY!

An Enid Blyton story
devised and adapted
by Mary Danby

Based on Enid Blyton's
Five Run Away Together

Illustrated by Kate Rogers

KNIGHT BOOKS
Hodder and Stoughton

Text copyright © 1987 Mary
Danby/Darrell Waters Limited
Illustrations copyright © 1987
Hodder and Stoughton Limited

*First published in Great Britain in
1988 by Knight Books*

Enid Blyton is a Trade Mark of
Darrell Waters Ltd

British Library C.I.P.

Danby, Mary
  Run away!: an Enid Blyton story.
  (The Famous five and you; 3).
  1. Adventure games – Juvenile
  literature
  I. Title II. Rogers, Kate
  III. Blyton, Enid. Five run away
  together IV. Series
  793'.9   GV1203

ISBN 0-340-42127-4

Printed and bound in Great Britain for
Hodder and Stoughton Paperbacks, a
division of Hodder and Stoughton
Limited, Mill Road, Dunton Green,
Sevenoaks, Kent TN13 2YA
(Editorial Office: 47 Bedford
Square, London WC1B 3DP) by
Cox and Wyman Limited, Reading,
Berks. Photoset by Rowland
Phototypesetting Limited,
Bury St Edmunds, Suffolk.

THE FAMOUS FIVE – AND YOU

Unlike an ordinary book, which you can read straight through from beginning to end, this is a gamebook, in which *you* choose how the story should go.

Begin at paragraph number 1. At the end of each paragraph you are told which paragraph to read next. Sometimes you will find you have a choice. (For instance, at the end of paragraph 8 you have to decide whether the Famous Five should drive past the bay or through the woods.)

Every time you have a choice to make, there will be one way that is the quickest and best – and you have to guess (or work out, if you can) which it is. If you choose the wrong paragraph, you can still carry on reading, but when you find yourself back at the main story you will find you have picked up a few 'red herrings'.

A red herring is the name given to something that carries you away from the main subject (as when someone is telling you a story and puts in all sorts of details that don't really matter). Your aim is to try and stay on the main track, without going off down the little side roads.

See if you can make the right choices and find your way to the end of the story without picking up too many red herrings. A red herring is shown by this symbol: ⌀ Use a pencil and paper to add up your score as you go along, then turn to the back of the book to see how well The Famous Five (and You) have done.

1

'George, dear, do settle down and do something,' said Georgina's mother. 'You keep wandering in and out with Timmy, and I'm trying to have a rest.'

'Sorry, Mother,' said George, who hated the name Georgina, 'but I feel lonely without the others.' She took hold of Timmy's collar. 'Oh, I do wish tomorrow would come.'

In the holidays George usually joined up with her cousin Anne, and Anne's two brothers Julian and Dick, and they had a lot of fun. The three cousins had been away with their parents, but they were coming to Kirrin Cottage the next day to spend the rest of their holidays with George.

Go to **5.**

2

'I think we should stop,' said Julian. 'If we're late home I'm sure Aunt Fanny will understand when we explain what happened.'

George pulled the pony cart to a halt, and Julian and Anne jumped down. They went over to the little boy.

'What's the matter? Are you lost?' asked Julian.

The little boy was crying too much to answer Julian, so Anne sat down beside him and put her arm around him. She pulled out her handkerchief and wiped his eyes.

'We want to help you,' she said. 'Can you tell us your name?'

The little boy sniffed and gulped. 'It's James,' he said in a whisper.

'And where do you live, James?' asked Anne.

Suddenly a girl of about sixteen came running out of the woods.

Go to **4.**

3

To their delight it was Aunt Fanny who stood at the back door.

'Welcome back to Kirrin Cottage, my dears,' she said. 'I'm so pleased to see you all again! Did you have a good journey? And how are your mother and father?'

'Hello, Aunt Fanny!' said Julian. 'Gosh, it's super to be back at Kirrin Cottage again! Mother and Father are fine, thank you. They send you their love.'

'How kind of them,' replied his aunt. 'Bring your things indoors. Uncle Quentin has gone out for a walk, I'm afraid, but he'll be back soon.'

The children looked at each other. They were quite relieved to find that their uncle was out!

Aunt Fanny suddenly put her hand to her head.

'Mother!' cried George. 'Are you feeling all right?'

Go to **11.**

4

She stopped when she saw Julian and Anne with the little boy.

'Oh, thank goodness!' she exclaimed breathlessly. 'James, what did you mean by wandering off like that? You gave me such a fright!'

'We were driving along the road and we heard this little boy crying,' said Anne. 'So we stopped to see if there was anything we could do to help.'

'That was very kind of you,' replied the girl. 'We were having a walk in the woods, and James ran after a squirrel, and I lost him. He's my little brother. Come on, James. Time to go home.'

The little boy trotted off happily with his sister, and Julian and Anne got back into the cart. George took up the reins, and soon they were out of the woods and climbing the hill behind the bay. They could see Kirrin Island lying quietly in the sunshine.

'Good old Kirrin Island,' said Julian. 'I can't wait to visit it again. When do you think we'll be able to go over there, George?'

'Well,' said George. 'I've got an idea.'

Go to **20.**

George decided to take Timmy down to the beach. She stood on the sand with him and looked out to the entrance of the bay. In the middle of it, almost as if it were guarding it, lay a small, rocky island, on which rose the ruins of an old castle.

I wish Mother would let us go and live on the island for a week, thought George. That would be the greatest fun we could have. To live on my very own island!

It *was* George's island. It really belonged to her mother, but she had said, two or three years back, that George could have it, and George now thought of it as her own.

Go to **8.**

The pony cart swung round a bend in the road, and there, sitting on the grass verge and crying his eyes out, was a small boy.

'Goodness!' said George. 'I wonder if he's all right? What is he doing sitting there all alone? He doesn't look more than four.'

'Perhaps we ought to stop,' suggested Anne. 'He may be lost.'

'I expect he's just fallen over. Someone will come and pick him up in a minute,' said Dick.

'Well,' said George, 'I don't want to be late home. Mother will worry. What do you think we should do, Julian?'

If you think they should stop, go to **2.**
If you think they should go on, go to **14.**

'What's Mrs Stick like?' asked Dick.

'I don't like her very much,' said George. 'She's got a horrible dog, too. It's a dreadful animal, smaller than Timmy, all sort of mangy and moth-eaten. I tried to make friends with it when Mrs Stick first arrived, but it nearly snapped one of my fingers off. Timmy can't bear it, either.'

'How is Uncle Quentin?' asked Anne. The three children didn't much like George's father because he could get into very fierce tempers sometimes.

'Father's all right,' said George cheerfully. 'Only he's a bit worried about Mother.'

A moment or two later she swung the pony cart into the back yard of Kirrin Cottage. The children jumped out eagerly and started to unload their suitcases. They looked up as the back door opened, hoping to see Aunt Fanny coming out to greet them.

If you think it's Aunt Fanny opening the door, go to **3**.
If you think it's someone else, go to **15**.

8

George went to meet her cousins the next day, driving the pony and trap to the station herself. Her mother wanted to come, but she said that she didn't feel very well. George was a bit worried about her. So often lately her mother hadn't been well. Perhaps it was the heat of the summer. The weather had been so hot lately. George was very sunburnt, and with her hair cut very short she really did look like a boy. She was pleased about this, because she had always wanted to be a boy.

The train came in. Three hands waved madly from a window, and George shouted in delight.

'Julian! Dick! Anne! You're here at last!'

The three children tumbled out of their carriage. Julian found a porter, who fetched their luggage from the guard's van.

There was a terrific noise as the four children all stood shouting their news at once, and Timmy barked without stopping. Then the porter wheeled up their cases, and they all went out to the station yard, where the pony cart was waiting. The suit-cases were loaded on to the back of the cart, the children climbed in, and they set off.

'It's a lovely day for a drive,' said George. 'Which way home would you like to take? The usual road past the bay, or the longer one that goes through the woods?'

If you think they should go past the bay, go to **12.**
If you think they should go through the woods, go to **17.**

9

'Oh, let's go for a swim, then,' said George. 'We can take Timmy for a walk later on.'

Down they went, the four of them, with Timmy galloping behind them, his tail wagging nineteen to the dozen. He went into the water with the children and swam all around them.

They dried themselves and pulled on their jeans and jerseys again. Then back to breakfast they went, as hungry as hunters. Anne noticed a boy in the back garden, and stared in surprise.

'Who's that?' she asked.

Go to **16.**

10

It was cool and pleasant driving through the woods. The sun was so hot that they were all quite glad to be in the shade of the trees for a while.

'How is your father, George?' asked Julian.

'Father's all right,' said George, 'but he's very busy, as usual. So be a bit careful of him at the moment. You know what he's like when he's busy.'

The children did know. Julian, Dick and Anne didn't like George's father very much because he could get into very fierce tempers, and although he welcomed the three cousins to his house he didn't really care for children.

Just then Anne thought she heard a noise.

'Listen!' she said. 'I think I can hear someone crying!'

Go to **6**.

11

Aunt Fanny gave a weak smile. 'No, I'm afraid I still feel rather odd,' she said. 'I think I'd better go and lie down again. I'm sorry about this, children, but Mrs Stick will help you get your things indoors. Go straight up and wash, then we'll have tea. I'm sure you're hungry!'

Aunt Fanny went back into the house, and a moment later a grim, sour-faced woman appeared and started to help them with their cases.

'Mrs Stick!' George whispered to Julian.

'Good name for her!' Julian replied with a grin. 'She looks a real old stick!'

Go to **24**.

'Oh, the road that goes past the bay,' said Dick, before anyone else could speak. 'I want to have a look at Kirrin Island again, and, anyway, I'm starving hungry! The sooner we get back to Kirrin Cottage for tea the better!'

So George turned the pony cart on to the road that led along the shore of the bay, and soon they could see Kirrin Island.

'Good old Kirrin Island,' said Julian. 'I can't wait to visit it again. When do you think we'll be able to go over there, George?'

'Well,' said George. 'I've got an idea.'

Go to **20**.

Julian and Anne set off down the road to Kirrin. They went down past Kirrin Cottage and had just reached the outskirts of Kirrin when a car suddenly roared past them, going very fast!

'That's the car that was stuck in the lane!' said Julian.

Go to **26**.

But before Julian had time to answer George, two women and several more children came out of the woods. One of the women picked up the little boy, who was rubbing his head as if it hurt.

'He must have fallen over and banged his head,' said Anne. 'He's all right now.'

The pony cart bowled on down the road, and soon they were out of the woods and climbing the hill behind the bay. They could see Kirrin Island lying quietly in the sunshine.

'Good old Kirrin Island,' said Julian. 'I can't wait to visit it again. When do you think we'll be able to go over there, George?'

'Well,' said George. 'I've got an idea.'

Go to **20.**

15

A sour-faced woman came out through the back door to help them down with their luggage. The children looked at one another. They didn't need George to tell them that this was Mrs Stick.

'She looks a real old stick!' said Julian with a grin, as he carried his case into the house.

George put the pony cart away, and the other three went to say hello to Aunt Fanny, who was lying down.

'Well, dears,' said Aunt Fanny. 'How are you all? I'm sorry I couldn't come to meet you. Uncle Quentin has gone out for a walk. You'd better go upstairs and wash straight away, then come and have tea.'

Go to **24.**

If you've arrived from **38**, *score three red herrings:* ⊂く
⊂く ⊂く.
If you've arrived from **26**, *score* ⊂く ⊂く ⊂く ⊂く.
If you've arrived from **21**, *score* ⊂く ⊂く ⊂く ⊂く ⊂く.

'Oh, that's Edgar, Mrs Stick's boy,' said George. 'I don't like him. He does silly things, like putting out his tongue and calling rude names.'

Edgar appeared to be singing when the others went in at the gate. Anne stopped to listen.

'Georgie-Porgie, pudding and pie!' sang Edgar, a silly look on his face. He seemed about thirteen or fourteen, a stupid, yet sly-looking boy. 'Georgie-Porgie, pudding and pie!'

George went red. 'He's always singing that,' she said furiously. 'Just because I'm called George, I suppose. He thinks he's clever. I can't bear him.'

Julian made a step towards Edgar, and he disappeared into the house at once.

Go to **23**.

'Oh, do let's go through the woods!' said Anne. 'I love driving in the pony cart.'

The others were quite happy to go home by the longer route, so George turned the pony down the narrow lane behind the station.

The pony trotted briskly along while the children caught up on all the news of the past weeks.

Anne and George had seen each other at school, of course, but George hadn't seen Julian and Dick since the end of the Easter holidays, so they all had a great deal to tell one another. Timmy sat on the seat beside George, barking from time to time to show how pleased he was to see everyone together again!

Go to **10**.

18

'I think it would be best if two of us go and look for the driver and two go for the police,' said Julian. 'Anne, you and I will go down to Kirrin and tell the police, and you and George can start searching the moors, Dick.'

'What shall we do if we don't find anything?' asked Dick.

'Go back to Kirrin Cottage and wait for us,' said Julian. 'If you do find anyone, and they need help, one of you stay with them, and one of you come and tell us. Right?'

'Right,' said George.

Go to **13**.

19

It was lovely to wake up the next morning at Kirrin Cottage and see the sun shining in at the windows, and to hear the far-off *plash-plash-plash* of the sea. It was gorgeous to leap out of bed and see how blue the sea was, and how lovely Kirrin Island looked at the entrance of the bay.

'Shall we have a swim before breakfast?' Julian asked Dick as they got out of bed.

Just then they heard George banging on the door.

'Come on, you two, get up!' she shouted. 'It's a lovely day, and I'm going to take Timmy for a walk before breakfast.'

Julian opened the door.

'We were thinking of going for a swim, actually,' he said. 'What do you think – shall we go for a swim or a walk?'

If you think they should go for a swim, go to **9.**
If you think they should go for a walk, go to **27.**

20

If you've arrived from **14,** *score three red herrings:* ⌒
⌒ ⌒.
If you've arrived from **4,** *score:* ⌒ ⌒ ⌒ ⌒.

'What sort of an idea?' asked Dick excitedly.

'I thought it would be marvellous if we could go and stay on Kirrin Island for a whole week by ourselves. I'm sure Mother would let us,' answered George.

'Go and stay on your island for a week!' cried Anne. 'Oh! That would be too good to be true.'

'Mother's not been feeling very well,' went on George, 'so I think she might be glad to have us out of the house for a while.'

'I hope Aunt Fanny isn't seriously ill,' said Julian, who was very fond of his aunt.

'I think it may be the heat,' said George. 'Anyway, we've had to get a housekeeper for a while to take care of the house until Mother's feeling better. Her name is Mrs Stick.'

Go to **7**.

21

'Now, do you want to come back to Kirrin Cottage with us and telephone the garage?' asked Dick.

'Or perhaps Mr Sanders at Kirrin Farmhouse could get his tractor and give you a tow,' suggested Julian.

'That's a good idea,' said Mr Walters. 'If you'll show me the path, I'll go to the farmhouse.'

The children escorted Mr Walters to the path that led over the moors to the farmhouse, then headed back towards Kirrin Cottage.

'We'd better hurry, otherwise we'll be late for breakfast,' said Anne.

'I'm starving,' said Dick.

'You're *always* starving,' said George with a laugh.

Soon they were back at the cottage. As they

walked in through the gate Anne noticed a boy in the back garden, and stared in surprise.

'Who's that?' she asked.

Go to **16.**

22

'I heard the milk lorry just after I woke up,' said George. 'That has to come down the lane, and it wouldn't have been able to get past this car. I'm sure it can't have been here very long.'

'Maybe the person who was driving it took a short cut across the moors,' suggested Anne. 'You can just see Kirrin Farmhouse, and perhaps the driver decided to ask for help there.'

'There isn't a path to Kirrin Farmhouse from here,' said George. 'Anyone crossing the moors off the path runs the risk of stepping into one of the boggy areas and not being able to get out!'

The children looked at each other.

'What shall we do?' asked Dick. 'Shall we go back to the village and ring the police, or shall we go and see if we can find anyone?'

'Perhaps two of us ought to go and ring the police, while the other two start to look,' suggested George.

If you think they should all go down to the village and ring the police, go to **30.**
If you think they should all go and look for the driver, go to **35.**

If you think two of them should go and look for the driver and two go to the police, go to **18.**

23

'Shan't stand much of *him*,' said Julian, as Edgar disappeared. 'I wonder *you* do, George. You used to be so fierce.'

'Well – I am still, really,' said George. 'But you see, Mother really hasn't been well, and I know jolly well that if I go for Edgar, Mrs Stick will leave. Then poor old Mother would have to do all the work, and she isn't fit for it at the moment. I think I'll just go up to her room and see if she'd like breakfast in bed.'

George went into the house. Suddenly a mangy-looking dog appeared out of the kitchen door. It had a dirty white coat, out of which patches seemed to have been bitten, and its tail was well between its legs.

'*Wooooof!*' said Timmy joyfully, and leapt at the dog. Julian caught his collar.

Go to **28.**

24

If you've arrived from **11**, *score one red herring:* ◁.

The boys carried their luggage up to their old bedroom, with its slanting roof and its window looking out over the bay. Anne went to the little room she shared with George. How good it was to

be back at Kirrin! What fun they would have these holidays with George and dear old Timmy!

Go to **19.**

25

How could they rescue him without getting stuck in the bog themselves?

'I wish we had a ladder,' said Julian. 'Or even a rope.'

'Wait a minute,' said George, who had been gazing thoughtfully at the tree. 'I've got an idea. See that branch there – the one that's sticking out over the mud pool? Well, if I climb up and wriggle along it, it will bend under my weight, and the man will be able to catch hold of the end of it. Then I'll wriggle back towards the trunk of the tree, and the branch will lift up and pull the man out!'

Julian looked at George, then looked at the tree.

'Right,' he called to the man, and explained George's plan. 'Ready, then?'

The man nodded, and George began to climb the tree.

Go to **32.**

26

'We'd better go and find the others, hadn't we?' suggested Anne. But as they ran back up the lane they saw George, Dick and Timmy flying down towards them.

'Did you see that car go past?' panted Dick.

'We hadn't gone very far on to the moors when we heard the sound of a car starting up,' said George. 'We ran back to the place where the car had been in the lane, and it was gone!'

'Obviously the driver came back,' said Julian. 'I wonder where he'd been, and what he'd been doing? He was driving terribly fast.'

'It's quite a mystery, isn't it?' said Dick. 'But there's nothing that we can do now, so we'd better get back to Kirrin Cottage for breakfast. I'm starving!'

'You're *always* starving,' said Anne with a laugh.

Soon they were back at the cottage. Anne

noticed a boy in the back garden and stared in surprise.

'Who's that?' she asked.

Go to **16.**

27

George thought for a moment. 'I vote we go for a walk,' she said. 'We can swim later on, when we feel hot. I'll go and tell Anne.'

But just then Anne appeared on the landing in jeans and T-shirt. The four of them ran downstairs and out into the garden, through the back gate and into the lane behind the house. Timmy galloped behind them, wagging his tail, his long pink tongue hanging out of his mouth.

The lane started to slope uphill, and, looking back, they could see the bay and the island.

'To think we may be able to spend a week over there on our own!' exclaimed Dick.

'That would be absolutely super,' agreed Julian. 'Hello, what's this?'

A car was parked in the lane, taking up so much space that there was no room for another car to get past it. The car was empty.

'What a stupid place to park a car!' said George scornfully. 'Nobody can get up or down the lane at all. What if Mr Sanders were to come along on his tractor? He'd have to reverse all the way back to the crossroads.'

'Perhaps the car has broken down,' suggested

Dick. 'And the person who was driving it has gone off to find a telephone.'

'But to get down to the village he would have to have walked along this lane,' said George. 'And we haven't seen anyone since we set off.'

'It's probably been here since before we came out for our walk,' said Julian.

Go to **22.**

28

Timmy pulled Julian over, for he was a big, strong dog, and the boy let go. Timmy pounced excitedly on the other dog, who gave a fearful whine and tried to go back through the kitchen door.

'Timmy! Come here at once!' yelled Julian. But Timmy didn't hear. He was busy trying to snap off the other dog's ears – or, at least, that's what he appeared to be doing. The other dog yelled for help.

Edgar now reappeared, looking very scared. He picked up a stone and seemed to be watching his chance to hurl it at Timmy. Anne shrieked.

'You're not to throw that stone. You're not to! You horrible boy!'

Edgar hesitated, the stone in his hand.

If you think Edgar throws the stone, go to **34.**
If you think he drops it, go to **39.**

'We thought we might go for a picnic,' said George eagerly. 'I asked Mother, and she said we might, if Mrs Stick will make us sandwiches.'

There was silence. Nobody liked the idea of asking Mrs Stick for sandwiches.

'I do wish she hadn't brought Stinker,' said George gloomily. 'Everything would be easier if he wasn't here.'

'I thought the dog was called Tinker,' said Uncle Quentin, startled.

'Well, Mrs Stick calls him Tinker, but I call him Stinker, because he really does smell awful,' said George with a grin.

Uncle Quentin got up from the table. 'Well, enjoy your morning. Be polite to Mrs Stick, won't you?' he said, and left the room.

'I've had an idea,' said Dick. 'Could we go into town and buy some postcards, and perhaps go to a café for some lemonade and buns? Then we won't have to ask Mrs Stick for sandwiches. What do you think?'

'I'd prefer a picnic,' said Anne.

If you think they should decide to have a picnic, go to **37.**
If you think they should decide to go into town, go to **40.**

'I think we had all better go to the police,' said Julian. 'If two of us were to go off and look for the driver, they could get lost too!'

Whistling to Timmy, who was half way down a rabbit hole with his tail wagging happily, they turned back the way they had come, past Kirrin Cottage and on down the road to Kirrin Village itself.

Sergeant Thompson was behind the desk as the children walked into the little police station.

'Why, good morning, George!' he said. 'I see your cousins are here again. Are they staying long?'

'For the rest of the holidays, I hope,' said George.

'Now, what can I do for you all?' asked the sergeant.

Go to **38.**

31

They looked at each other in dismay.

'We'll just have to go home,' said George. 'Perhaps we can have our picnic after all.'

'But that means somebody will have to ask Mrs Stick for sandwiches,' objected Dick. 'We can't have a picnic without sandwiches!'

They walked back up the hill to Kirrin Cottage and stopped in the garden, trying to decide who was going to ask Mrs Stick to make the sandwiches.

'This is ridiculous,' said Julian. 'She isn't going to bite us!'

'No, but her horrid dog might,' said Anne. 'I'm certainly not going into the kitchen!'

Go to **37**.

32

In no time George was inching her way along the branch. Slowly, the end of it started to bend and, when she was half way along, the man was able to grab the end of the branch in both hands.

'Right, George!' shouted Julian. 'Back you go!'

George began to wriggle back towards the trunk of the tree, and very slowly the end of the branch started to rise. The children watched anxiously. Then suddenly, just as George reached the trunk, the end of the branch came up with a rush, there was a loud sucking noise, and the man's legs came free. He threw himself at the side of the mud pool. As he did so, the branch snapped, and he landed with the end of it in his hands!

'Are you all right?' asked Anne.

'Oh, yes, I think so,' said the man. 'I've got very wet and muddy legs, but thanks to you four I'm fine otherwise. My goodness, I should have been in trouble if you hadn't come along!'

George climbed down the tree.

'My car's broken down – you may have seen it back there in the lane,' the man went on. 'I was trying to get to that farmhouse to ring for help,' he explained. 'My name is Walters, by the way. Who are you?'

'I'm Julian, and these are my brother Dick and my sister Anne, and my cousin George, and the dog is Timmy,' said Julian.

'You're quite a boy,' said Mr Walters to George. 'Thank you very much!'

George beamed at him. She was delighted to have been mistaken for a boy!

Go to **21**.

33

If you've come from **46**, *score* ⌣ ⌣.

Breakfast was rather a subdued meal, as Aunt Fanny wasn't there and Uncle Quentin was – and Uncle Quentin in a bad temper wasn't a very cheerful person to have at the breakfast table. He snapped at George and glared at the others.

However, by the time breakfast was over he was feeling a little better, and didn't like to see such subdued faces around him.

'What are you going to do today?' he asked the children.

Go to **29**.

34

Seeing that Julian was busy trying to separate the two dogs, Edgar threw his stone at Timmy. Timmy gave a startled yelp and let go of the other dog, which immediately started to run back towards the kitchen. But Timmy was too quick for him. He pounced on the other dog again, and they rolled over and over on the grass, growling and biting.

Julian had seen Edgar throw the stone and he was furiously angry.

'You absolute beast!' he yelled, and launched himself at Edgar.

Edgar, taken by surprise, fell over on the lawn. Julian landed on top of him and began to pummel Edgar for all he was worth. Between the two dogs and the two boys fighting, the noise in the garden was terrible!

Go to **42.**

35

'I think we should all go and look for the driver,' said Julian. 'We can fan out over the moors and cover quite a large area. If he's got stuck in one of the boggy places he'll need help.'

So they set off across the moors, treading very carefully. Timmy ran on in front of them. Just as they came to the top of a slight rise, they heard someone shouting: 'Help! Help!'

'That could be the driver!' exclaimed Dick.

'Where are you?' shouted Julian.

'Over here,' the voice shouted back. 'Under the tree!'

Looking around, the children spotted a large tree away to their left.

'Come on!' said Julian, and he started to run.

In no time at all they had reached the tree. A man was up to his waist in mud a short distance away from it.

'Thank goodness you've come,' he said. 'I can't get out of here. Can you help me?'

Go to **25.**

36

Just then Jim the boatman appeared.

'Hello, George,' he said. 'Timmy hurt himself, has he?'

'No,' said George. 'He's got paint on his paws. I thought that the boat was dry, and we could go for a row. I told Timmy to get in, but the inside of the boat was still wet. How can I get the paint off his paws?'

'It won't wash off,' said Jim. 'I'll have to go and get some turpentine. That'll do it.'

'Won't it sting his paws?' asked Anne.

'No, I don't think so,' replied Jim. 'But if you make him go for a swim after I've cleaned his paws the sea water will wash the turps off. Just hold on to him until I get back. If he runs around on the beach the sand will stick to his paws and he'll be in a terrible mess!'

Go to **53.**

If you've come from **31**, *score* ◁ ◁ ◁.

In the end it was Aunt Fanny who saw Mrs Stick. Mrs Stick went up to see Aunt Fanny, who was still in bed, and agreed to make the sandwiches, though with a very bad grace.

'I didn't bargain for three more children to come traipsing along,' she said sulkily.

'I told you they were coming, Mrs Stick,' said Aunt Fanny patiently. 'I didn't know I should be feeling so ill myself when they came. If I'd been well I could have made their sandwiches myself.'

The children took their packets of sandwiches and set off. On the way they met Edgar.

'Why don't you let me come along with you?' he said. 'Let's go to that island. I know a lot about it, I do.'

Julian winked at the others.

'Yes, Edgar, of course you can come with us!' he said.

But George hadn't seen the wink.

'No! We don't want you anywhere near us!' she retorted.

If Edgar goes with them, go to **41**.
If he stays at home, go to **45**.

'We found what looks like an abandoned car in the lane behind Kirrin Cottage,' said Julian. 'There was no sign of the driver, and nothing can get up or down past the car – it's blocking the whole lane.'

'Well, we can't have that,' said Sergeant Thompson. 'I'll send a constable up to move it and see if there's any sign of the driver.'

'I think we ought to get back to Kirrin Cottage for breakfast,' said George as they came out into the sunshine again.

'Goodness, I'm starving!' exclaimed Dick.

As they walked in through the gate Anne noticed a boy in the back garden, and stared in surprise.

'Who's that?' she asked.

Go to **16.**

39

Edgar dropped the stone and stood glaring at the children. Then Uncle Quentin appeared looking angry and irritable.

'Good heavens! What is all this going on? I never heard such a row in my life.'

George came flying out of the door like the wind, to rescue her beloved Timmy. She rushed to the two dogs and tried to pull Timmy away. Her father yelled at her.

'Come away, you little idiot! Don't you know better than to separate two fighting dogs with your bare hands? Where's the garden hose?'

It was fixed to a tap nearby. Julian ran to it and turned on the tap. He picked up the hose and aimed it at the two dogs. At once the jet of water spurted out at them, and they leapt apart in surprise.

'Now, George,' said Uncle Quentin, 'tie Timmy up at once. Edgar, take your dog into the kitchen. And tell your mother that I would like breakfast immediately!'

Edgar and the dog disappeared back into the kitchen, and George, looking sulky, tied Timmy up.

Go to **33**.

40

'I think it would be a good idea to go to town this morning,' said Julian. 'After all, we did promise to send Mother and Father a postcard. We might be able to have a picnic tea on the beach instead.'

'There's a bus at about half-past ten,' said George. 'We'll catch that, shall we?'

So after breakfast they set off down the road to Kirrin, Timmy running on ahead of them.

'Will they allow Timmy on the bus, George?' asked Anne.

'Oh, yes, provided I keep him off the seats,' said George. 'I quite often take him into town with me.'

They reached the bus-stop and settled down on a bench to wait for the bus.

Go to **44**.

'Oh, come on, George!' said Julian, grinning at her and winking again. 'Let Edgar come with us if he wants to.'

George realised that Julian must be up to something. She hesitated for a moment, then said reluctantly, 'Oh, all right.'

Edgar was very pleased, and walked along behind the others with a silly grin on his face. He was careful to keep well away from Timmy, though.

'What time do you think we'll be having lunch?' he asked.

'*We'll* be having lunch at about one o'clock,' said Julian. 'What about you, Edgar?'

'I'll be having lunch at the same time as you, of course,' replied Edgar.

'Oh, really?' said Julian. 'Where are your sandwiches, then?'

Go to **47**.

42

In the middle of all the turmoil Uncle Quentin appeared, looking angry and irritable.

'Good heavens! What is all this going on? I never heard such a row in my life!'

Then George appeared, flying out of the door like the wind, to rescue her beloved Timmy. She rushed to the two dogs and tried to pull Timmy away. Her father yelled at her.

'Come away, you little idiot! Don't you know better than to separate two fighting dogs with your bare hands? Where's the garden hose?'

It was fixed to a tap nearby. Uncle Quentin ran to it and turned on the tap. He picked up the hose and turned it on the two dogs.

Go to **46.**

43

'It certainly looks dry enough to me,' said Dick.

George ran her finger along the outside of the boat. The paint really did feel dry.

'Oh, come on,' she said. 'I must say I'd like to use my boat again. It's ages since I went for a row. Come on, Timmy!'

Timmy jumped into the boat and made his way to the bow, where he liked to stand. Then suddenly he bent down and began to lick one of his feet.

'What's the matter, Timmy?' asked George. 'Have you got a thorn in your paw? Come here and let me have a look.'

Timmy jumped out of the boat, and George picked up his front paw.

'Oh, goodness,' she said. 'Don't anyone else get in the boat! Timmy's paws are covered in paint!'

'How are we going to get it off?' asked Anne.

Go to **36.**

44

After about a quarter of an hour, Dick looked at his watch.

'The bus is rather late, isn't it? It's past twenty to eleven already! I wonder where it can be?' he said.

Just then Sergeant Thompson came along on his bike and saw the children waiting at the bus-stop.

'Hello,' he said. 'What are you all doing here?'

'We're waiting for the bus into town,' explained George.

'But there isn't a half-past ten bus any more,' said Sergeant Thompson. 'The bus company stopped it about six weeks ago. The next bus isn't until two o'clock!'

Go to **31**.

45

'And you don't know anything about my island, either!' continued George. 'It belongs to *me*! We should never allow you to visit it.'

''Tisn't your island,' said Edgar. 'That's a lie, that is!'

'You don't know what you're talking about,' said George scornfully. 'Come on, you lot! We can't waste time talking to Edgar.'

They left him, looking sulky and angry.

'Let's go and see if your boat is ready,' said

Julian. 'Then maybe we could row out to the dear old island.'

Go to **50.**

46

At once the jet of water spurted out at the two fighting dogs, and they leapt apart in surprise. Then Uncle Quentin swung around and directed the hose on Julian and Edgar, who were still struggling on the ground. They were about the same height, but Julian was stronger and fitter than the overweight Edgar, and he definitely had the upper hand. The two boys rolled apart when the water hit them, then got to their feet, panting. They were both soaking wet.

'Go back into the house, Edgar, and take your dog with you. Tell your mother I shall expect breakfast to be ready in ten minutes,' ordered Uncle Quentin. He turned to Julian. 'I'm ashamed of you, Julian. I thought you'd know better. Really, if you're going to behave like this I shall seriously have to consider sending you home. I cannot have these disruptions to my work!'

He turned and strode angrily into the house.

Go to **33.**

Edgar stared at Julian.

'Ain't got no sandwiches,' he muttered. 'You'll have to share yours with me.'

Julian shook his head.

'Oh, no, we won't,' he said. 'Your mother only made a few sandwiches for us – there won't be enough to give you any!'

'Go on!' shouted Edgar. 'I don't believe you. My mum always gives me plenty to eat. Of course you've got enough sandwiches to share with me!'

'I'd say Edgar's mother gives him a great deal too much to eat,' Dick murmured to Anne. 'He's terribly plump and unhealthy.'

Anne giggled. It was true; Edgar was fat and pasty-looking.

'Well, your mother has barely given us enough for ourselves,' said Julian. 'So if you come with us, I'm afraid you'll have to do without any lunch!'

Go to **54.**

Go to **54.**

48

'No,' said George. 'I don't think so. It's on the rocks on the other side of the island you remember, so we can't see it from here. But we might have a look at it when we go to the island tomorrow.'

They walked along the beach with Timmy capering ahead of them. They could see the island clearly, with the ruined castle rising up from the middle.

'Hello!' said Julian suddenly. 'What's that over there on the island?'

Everyone gazed hard at Kirrin Island. George gave an exclamation.

'Golly – it looks like a sort of spire of smoke! Surely it's smoke! Someone's on my island. Or, rather, *our* island,' she corrected herself, for she felt the island belonged to all four of them – and Timmy, too.

'There couldn't be anyone there, surely,' said Dick. 'That smoke must come from a steamer out beyond the island. We can't see it, that's all.'

'If we climb the cliff we may be able to see a bit more,' suggested Julian.

'I don't know,' said George doubtfully. 'The cliffs aren't very safe just here. We could walk further along the beach. We'll be able to see a bit more of the island if we do that.'

If you think they should climb the cliff, go to **52.**
If you think they should walk further along the beach, go to **64.**

49

'What do you mean?' said George, suddenly feeling rather scared. 'Where's my mother?'

'Call her too, if you like,' said Edgar, looking sly. 'Go on! Call her.'

'Where are they? Where have my father and mother gone?' demanded George furiously. 'Tell me, you beast!'

'Find out for yourself,' said Edgar, grinning. 'They're certainly not here!'

'You're lying,' said George through clenched teeth. 'I'm going up to Mother's room to see if she's there!'

'I don't think we should let Edgar get away with this, George,' said Julian. 'We should *make* him tell us what's happened.'

If you think George should go straight up to her mother's room, go to **55.**

If you think they should make Edgar tell them what's happened, go to **63.**

50

If you've arrived from **54,** *score* ◠ ◠.

'I'm not sure if the boat's finished,' said George. 'Jim the boatman has been repainting it, you know.'

When they arrived at the beach, there was George's boat. It looked very cheerful, for George had chosen a bright red paint, and the oars were painted red too.

'It *looks* finished,' said Dick. 'Let's row over to the island.'

'Wait a minute, Dick,' said George. 'I know that it looks all right, but the paint may still be tacky. We don't want to get paint all over our clothes. Think how Mrs Stick would complain!'

Dick touched the outside of the boat with his finger.

'Look!' he said, holding it up. 'There's no paint on my finger. I'm sure it's dry. *Do* let's go for a row, George.'

George hesitated. 'We really ought to wait until I've asked Jim if it's ready,' she said.

If you think they should try the boat, go to **43.**
If you think they should wait for Jim, go to **57.**

51

If you've arrived from **61,** *score* ◁▷ ◁▷.

They turned to go back, watching Kirrin Island as they walked, but all they could see were jackdaws or gulls in the sky above it. No more spires of smoke appeared.

'The smoke must have come from a steamer, out of our sight behind the island,' suggested Dick.

'All the same, I'm going over tomorrow to have a look,' said George firmly. 'If any trippers are visiting our island I'll turn them off.'

When they got back to Kirrin Cottage, George noticed that the car wasn't there.

'Father must be out,' she said. 'I wonder if he'll be back for tea?'

They walked into the hall, then heard someone sneeze.

'Who's that?' said Julian.

'It sounded as though it came from the sitting-room,' said Anne.

'I thought it came from the study,' said George. 'And look, the study door is open. Father *always* closes the study door.'

'I don't think we'd better look in the study,' said Anne. 'You know Uncle Quentin doesn't like us going in there. Let's see if there's anyone in the sitting-room.'

'I think it would be a good idea to have a look in the study,' said George, frowning. 'It might be an intruder, and all Father's things are in there.'

If you think they should look in the sitting-room, go to **59**.
If you think they should check the study, go to **66**.

52

'Oh, come on,' said Julian. 'Let's climb the cliff. It'll be all right if we're careful. After all, if there is someone on the island we jolly well ought to know about it.'

'I've got an idea,' said Dick. 'Perhaps just one of us could climb up and have a look, while the rest wait here. Anyway, somebody will have to stay with Timmy. He won't be able to get up that cliff.'

'That's a good idea, Dick,' said Julian. 'You three stay here with Timmy, and I'll climb up and see what's going on.'

The cliff wasn't very high at that point, but it was composed of chalky rock, which crumbled easily. Julian made his way up slowly and carefully, testing each hand- and foot-hold. Eventually, to the relief of the three children watching on the beach, he reached the top of the cliff and wriggled on to the grass. He stood up and had a look at the island.

'I can't see anything,' he called down to the others, after staring hard at the island for a moment or two. 'No, there's no one there. I'm coming down now.'

Go to **58.**

53

George hung on to Timmy's collar while they waited for Jim to get the turps. He was back in five minutes with a small bottle and a rag. Timmy stood patiently while Jim cleaned all the paint off his feet, and when Jim had finished Timmy licked his hand as if to say thank you!

'There you are, George!' said Jim. 'Take him down to the sea now to wash his paws. He'll be fine.'

The four children walked down to the edge of the sea and let Timmy frolic through the waves.

'We'll go to the island tomorrow, then,' said Julian. 'We'll just picnic on the beach today. Then we can go for a walk.'

So they picnicked on the sands with Timmy sharing more than half their lunch. The sandwiches weren't very nice, but Timmy didn't mind. He gobbled up as many as he could, his tail wagging so hard that it sent sand over everyone.

Go to **60**.

54

Edgar stood still in the middle of the road for a moment. Meanwhile the others walked on, all secretly hoping that the thought of not having any lunch would make Edgar change his mind about going on their picnic.

And it did! Edgar turned around and started to walk back up the hill to Kirrin Cottage, scuffing his feet along the ground as he went.

'That's got rid of him!' said Julian with satisfaction. 'I thought he wouldn't want to come if he wasn't going to get anything to eat.'

'Let's go and see if your boat is ready, George,'

said Dick. 'Then maybe we could row out to the dear old island.'

Go to **50**.

55

'No, I'm going up to see if Mother is in her room,' said George, and she rushed out. The others heard her flying up the stairs, shouting loudly.

'Mother! Mother! Where are you?'

But her mother's bed was empty. George flew into all the other bedrooms, shouting desperately: 'Mother! Mother! Father! Where are you?'

But there was no answer. George ran downstairs, her face very white.

Edgar grinned up at her. 'What did I tell you?' he said.

'Where are they?' demanded George.

Then suddenly Timmy growled very loudly. He didn't like the way Edgar was looking at George. He bared his teeth, and the hackles on his neck stood up. He looked very frightening.

'Keep that dog away from me,' said Edgar, his voice trembling.

Julian put his hand on Timmy's collar. 'Quiet, Timmy!' he said. 'Now, Edgar, tell us what we want to know, or you'll be sorry!'

Go to **69**.

Julian and Dick had both thought that they might have to go home now that Aunt Fanny was in hospital, and neither of them liked the idea at all! It would mean poor George would be left on her own with Mrs Stick, for one thing, and they'd have to give up their idea of spending a week on Kirrin Island, too.

Just then Mrs Stick came into the sitting-room.

'Your father said to tell you,' she informed George, 'that your mother is very ill, and that he'll be staying with her until he's sure she's getting better. It may take two or three days, or longer. He'll ring every morning at nine o'clock to see how you are.' She paused, then added: 'And I must say I didn't bargain on having to look after a tribe of kids on my own!'

She went out of the room, slamming the door. George's eyes filled with tears.

'I can't bear Mother going away like this!' she sobbed, and buried her head in the cushions.

Go to **65.**

57

Just then Jim appeared.

'Oh, Jim, is my boat ready for us to use? The paint looks dry,' said George.

Jim shook his head. 'No, George,' he said. 'Not unless you all want to be messed up with red paint. It'll be dry tomorrow, but not before.'

'We'll go to the island tomorrow, then,' said Julian. 'We'll just picnic on the beach today. Then we can go for a walk.'

So they picnicked on the sands, with Timmy sharing more than half their lunch. The sandwiches weren't very nice. The bread was too stale, there wasn't enough butter, and they were far too thick. But Timmy didn't mind. He gobbled up as many as he could, his tail wagging so hard that it sent sand over everyone.

Go to **60.**

58

The others watched as Julian began to feel his way carefully down the cliff. Little bits of chalk kept breaking away from the cliff face and sliding down to the beach, but Julian climbed steadily down.

'Oh, do be careful, Julian!' Anne called anxiously.

At that moment Julian, distracted by Anne, missed his footing and came tumbling down the rest of the cliff on to the beach! He lay in a heap on the sand, not moving.

Go to **61.**

If you've arrived from **66**, *score* ◯↱.

'Let's try the sitting-room,' said Julian.

To their great surprise Edgar was in there, reading one of Julian's books.

'What are you doing here?' asked Julian. 'And who told you you could borrow my book?'

'I'm not doing any harm,' said Edgar. 'If I want to have a quiet read, why shouldn't I?'

'You wait until my father comes in and finds you lolling about here,' said George. 'My goodness, if you'd gone into his study you'd have been sorry.'

'I've been in there,' said Edgar surprisingly. 'I've seen those funny instruments he's working with.'

'So that's why the door was open!' exclaimed Dick.

'How *dare* you!' said George, going white with anger. 'Why, even *we* are not allowed in to my father's study. As for touching his things – well! I'm going to find him and get him to deal with you.'

'Call him if you like,' said Edgar. 'He won't come.'

Go to **49**.

If you've arrived from **53**, *score* ◠ ◠.

'Timmy, do take your tail out of the sand if you want to wag it,' said Julian, getting sand all over his hair for the fourth time. Timmy wagged his tail hard again and sent another shower over Julian. Everyone laughed.

'Let's go for a walk now,' said Dick, jumping up. 'Where shall we go?'

'We'll walk along the cliff-top, where we can see the island all the time, shall we?' said Anne. 'George, is the old wreck still there?'

George nodded. The children had once had a most exciting time with an old wreck that had lain at the bottom of the sea. A great storm had lifted it up and set it firmly on the rocks. They had been able to explore the wreck then, and had found a map of Kirrin Castle in it, with instructions as to where hidden treasure was to be found.

'Isn't the wreck battered to pieces yet, George?' asked Julian.

Go to **48**.

61

George, Dick and Anne stood paralysed with horror for a moment, then rushed over to where Julian was lying.

'Julian! Julian!' cried Anne. 'Are you all right?'

Much to the relief of the others, Julian sat up

slowly and looked at them. He gave a shaky laugh.

'I'm fine,' he said. 'Or at least I think I am! All the breath was knocked out of me for a minute.'

'Try to stand up,' suggested George. 'You might have twisted your ankle or something.'

Julian got to his feet and took a couple of steps.

'No,' he said. 'I've grazed the palms of my hands and my arms, and I bumped my knee when I landed, but it doesn't hurt to walk, so I don't think I've broken anything.'

'It's lucky you were most of the way down,' said George. 'If that had happened while you were near the top of the cliff you might have been killed!'

'Oh, don't say that!' said Anne, her eyes filling with tears.

'Don't cry,' said Julian, putting his arm around his sister. 'I'm all right, really I am. And I think we'd better go home now. It's almost teatime.'

'I hope Mother will be up,' said George. 'It's much nicer when she's at meals.'

Go to **51.**

62

Julian looked all around the room, but he could see no sign of a note.

'I'll go and check the study,' he said. 'Perhaps Uncle Quentin left it in there.'

But there was no note in the study either. The children searched everywhere in the house that they could think of, but there was no sign of a note.

'It seems very strange that Father should just go off like this without saying *anything*,' said George.

'Perhaps he had to leave in such a hurry that there wasn't time to write us a note,' suggested Anne. 'He'll probably phone us later. Oh dear, I do hope this won't mean we have to go home!'

Go to **56.**

63

The four children grouped themselves around Edgar, who was still lolling in a chair.

'Now then, Edgar,' said Julian. 'What's happened? Where are George's father and mother?'

'I'm not going to tell you,' said Edgar. 'And if you hit me I'll tell my mother, and then she'll make you sorry.'

'Oh, no, Edgar,' said Julian, shaking his head slowly. 'You are the one who is going to be sorry, especially when we tell Uncle Quentin that you have been messing around in his study!'

Go to **72.**

64

'All right,' said Julian. 'If the cliffs aren't safe I certainly don't want to climb them.'

They walked along the beach, watching Kirrin Island carefully, but they could see no more smoke.

'If only my boat were ready,' said George restlessly, 'I'd go over this afternoon. I've a good mind to go and get it, even if the paint *is* wet!'

'Don't be an idiot!' said Julian. 'You know what an awful row we'd get into if we went home with our clothes covered in paint. Have a bit of sense, George! Anyway, I think we'd better get back home. It's almost teatime.'

'I hope Mother will be up,' said George. 'It's much nicer when she's at meals.'

Go to **51.**

65

If you've arrived from **56,** *score* ◯◁ ◯◁.

Julian sat down beside George and put his arm around her. 'Cheer up, George!' he said. 'Your mother will be all right, you wait and see!'

He got up and went to the door.

'I'm going to tell Mrs Stick that we want our tea,' he said.

Julian went into the kitchen. Edgar was sitting there, looking rather sulky, and Mrs Stick looked grim.

'You four kids leave my Edgar alone,' she said. 'If I have any nonsense from you I won't get you any meals, so just remember that!'

'And if we have any nonsense from you I shall go to the police,' said Julian unexpectedly. He hadn't meant to say that, but it had a surprising effect.

Go to **71.**

The four children went into the study and looked around. Since they were not allowed in Uncle Quentin's study, it was difficult to know if everything was in its usual place, but the window was closed and there didn't seem to be anything wrong.

George tiptoed over to the table where her father's test-tubes and instruments were laid out. 'These look all right,' she said. 'I don't think anything has been knocked over, and nothing's broken.'

'It's odd that the door was open, though,' said Anne. 'Uncle Quentin is so fussy about it always being closed.'

Go to **59.**

'Well, if Mrs Stick won't get our meals, we'll have to get them ourselves,' said George. 'I hate Mrs Stick. I hate that horrid Spotty-Face Edgar too, and that awful Stinker!'

'Look!' said Dick suddenly. 'There *is* Stinker.' He put out his hand to catch Timmy, who had risen with a growl, but Timmy shook off his hand and leapt at Stinker.

Just then Mrs Stick appeared with a piece of wood and lashed out at Timmy. Fortunately she missed. Tinker at once hurled himself at Mrs Stick and tried to hide behind her skirt, trembling with terror.

'I'll poison that dog of yours!' said Mrs Stick furiously to George, and she disappeared indoors again.

Just then the telephone rang. George jumped up. 'I expect that's Father!' she said.

'Well, it might be my mother,' said Julian. 'She did say she'd ring to see how we were.'

If you think it's Uncle Quentin on the phone, go to **74**.
If you think it's Julian's mother, go to **82**.

68

If you've arrived from **75**, *score* ◁.

Julian picked up the meat pie and the dish of tarts and made his way carefully out of the larder. He pushed the door closed with his foot. Then he turned to go out of the kitchen.

But in the dark he went the wrong way, and by bad luck walked straight into the sofa! The dish of tarts got a sudden jerk, and one of them fell off. It landed on the open mouth of the sleeping man.

The man sat up with a jump.

'Who's there? That you, Edgar? What are you doing down here?' He leapt up, lurched over to the light switch and turned it on, then stared at Julian in astonishment. 'What are you doing here?' he demanded.

'Just what I was about to ask *you*,' said Julian

coolly. 'What do you think *you're* doing here, in my uncle's kitchen?'

'I've a right to be here,' said the man rudely. 'My wife is cook here, and my ship's in and I'm on leave.'

Julian had feared as much. How awful to have three Sticks in the house!

'I'm going to speak to my uncle about you in the morning,' he said, and walked out of the kitchen.

Go to **73.**

69

'There isn't much to tell,' said Edgar, keeping his eye on Timmy. 'Your mother was suddenly taken very ill – with a terrible pain in her stomach – and they got the doctor and she was taken away to hospital, and your father went with her. That's all!'

George sat down on the sofa, looking pale and sick.

'Oh!' she said. 'Poor Mother! I wish I hadn't gone out today., Oh dear – how can we find out what's happened?'

'Perhaps your father left a note for us,' suggested Dick. 'Or maybe he'll ring us later.'

If you think there is a note, go to **81.**
If not, go to **62.**

Mrs Stick was in such a bad temper that evening that there was no supper at all. The four children were very hungry by then, so in the end they decided that one of them would have to go to the kitchen and ask for something to eat.

'I'll go,' said Julian. 'I don't like Mrs Stick, but I'm not afraid of her – nor her awful son!'

He walked down the passage to the kitchen. He could hear noises coming from within, so obviously Mrs Stick was in there. Julian turned the door handle.

If you think the door opens, go to **77.**
If you think it's locked, go to **85.**

Mrs Stick looked startled and alarmed. 'Now, there's no call to be nasty,' she said in a much more polite voice. 'We've all had a bit of a shock, and we're upset, like. I'll get your tea straight away.'

Julian went out of the kitchen. He wondered why his threat of going to the police had made Mrs Stick so agreeable. Perhaps she was afraid the police would contact Uncle Quentin, and he would come back and dismiss her.

After tea the children sat in the garden, keeping an ear open in case the telephone should ring.

From the kitchen came a song:

'Georgie-Porgie, pudding and pie,
Sat herself down and had a good cry,
Georgie-Porgie . . .'

Go to **78.**

Edgar turned pale. He was scared of Uncle Quentin.

'If you tell him that I was in his study, *I'll* tell him that you're lying – that it was one of you!' said Edgar after a moment.

'That's no good, Edgar,' said Julian. '*We* all know that Uncle Quentin doesn't like us to go into his study, and Uncle Quentin knows that we wouldn't disobey him – or tell lies! So that won't work!'

Go to **76.**

Upstairs, as they all sat around and ate the pie and the tarts, Julian told the others about Mr Stick coming on leave from his ship. Then, no longer hungry, they fell asleep.

In the morning, to their surprise, Mrs Stick actually produced some sort of breakfast. Afterwards Julian suggested a quick run down to the beach and back. Uncle Quentin was due to ring at nine and they didn't want to miss his call. When they came back they heard the telephone ringing. George dashed to answer it just as Mrs Stick came out of the kitchen and hurried towards the telephone.

Who answers the phone?
If you think Mrs Stick does, go to **80**.
If you think George does, go to **86**.

If you've arrived from **88**, *score* ◠ ◠.

George flew indoors and picked up the receiver.

'Is that you, George?' said her father. 'Are you all right?'

'Father – what about Mother? Tell me quickly – how is she?' asked George.

'We shan't know until the day after tomorrow,' said her father. 'I'll telephone tomorrow morning and then the next morning too, but I shan't come back until I know she's better.'

'Oh, Father – it's awful without you and Mother,' said poor George. 'Mrs Stick is so horrid.'

'Now, George,' said her father impatiently, 'surely you can make do with Mrs Stick until I get back! Don't bother me with such things. I've got enough to worry about as it is.'

'Can I come to see Mother?' asked George.

'No, not for at least two weeks, I'm afraid,' said her father. 'I'll be back as soon as I can, but I'm not going to leave your mother now. She needs me. Goodbye, and be good, all of you.'

George turned to face the others.

'Shan't know about Mother until the day after tomorrow,' she said. 'And we've got to put up with Mrs Stick until Father comes back. It's awful, isn't it?'

Go to **70.**

75

Julian shot out of the larder and looked around the room. There had to be someone there! But where?

And then he heard the coughing sound again. It seemed to be coming from the big kitchen sofa, which faced the stove and had its back towards Julian. He tiptoed over to the sofa and peeped over the back.

There was a small man lying on the sofa. He was fast asleep, his mouth wide open. He wasn't a very pleasant sight. He hadn't shaved for some days, and his chin was bluish-black. He had untidy hair and a nose just like Edgar's.

Must be dear Edgar's father! thought Julian. What a sight!

Quickly he snapped off the light and crept back to the larder. He felt along the shelves for the meat pie and jam tarts.

Go to **68.**

76

Edgar bit his lip and stared at the floor. At last he looked up at George.

'There isn't much to tell,' he said. 'Your mother was suddenly taken very ill – with a terrible pain in her stomach – and they got the doctor and she's been taken to hospital, and your father went with her. That's all!'

George sat down on the sofa, looking pale and sick.

'Oh!' she said. 'Poor Mother! I wish I hadn't gone out today. Oh dear – how can we find out what's happened?'

'Perhaps your father left a note for us,' suggested Dick. 'Or maybe he'll ring us later.'

If you think there is a note, go to **81.**
If not, go to **62.**

The kitchen door opened. Edgar and Mrs Stick were sitting at the table, finishing their supper.

'We'd like some supper, please, Mrs Stick,' said Julian.

'Oh, would you,' replied Mrs Stick. 'Well, you're not getting any, see? I don't like the way you kids have been behaving towards me and my Edgar, not to mention poor Tinker! You can all go to bed hungry, and maybe that will teach you to behave a bit better tomorrow. Now, go on, get out!'

She left the table and gave Julian a shove through the kitchen doorway. Then she slammed the door, and Julian heard the key turn in the lock.

Go to **85**.

78

Julian got up. He went to the kitchen window and looked in. Edgar was there alone.

'Can't you find anything better to do than sing nasty little songs about a girl who is miserable?' said Julian.

Edgar didn't stir. 'Can't I sing if I want to?' he asked. *'Georgie-Porgie . . .'*

But he didn't get any further. Julian reached in through the window and put his hand firmly over Edgar's mouth.

'Shut up, Spotty-Face!' he said furiously. 'Just shut up!'

Just then Mrs Stick came hurrying into the kitchen.

'You leave my Edgar alone!' she shouted when she saw what Julian was doing. She flew at him, and Julian withdrew his arm. 'How dare you!' she shrieked. 'You stop bullying my Edgar, or it'll be the worse for you, you mark my words!'

Leaving Mrs Stick fuming in the kitchen, Julian went back to the others.

'I'm afraid the fat's in the fire now,' he said, sitting down on the grass. 'We'll be lucky if we get any meals at all – it's open warfare between us and Mrs Stick!'

Go to **67.**

79

The kitchen was flooded with radiance, and Julian's eyes fastened on the figure of a small man lying on the sofa. He was fast asleep, his mouth wide open.

He wasn't a very pleasant sight. He hadn't shaved for some days, and his cheeks and chin were bluish-black. He had untidy hair and a nose exactly like Edgar's.

Must be dear Edgar's father, thought Julian. Then his stomach rumbled fiercely, so he snapped the light off again and crept towards the larder. He opened the door and felt along the shelves. Ah –

that felt like a pie of some sort. He lifted it up and sniffed. A meat pie – good!

He felt along the shelf again and came to a plate on which were what he thought must be jam tarts, for they were round and flat with something sticky in the middle.

Go to **68.**

80

If you've arrived from **86,** *score* $\bigcirc$⌐.

Mrs Stick picked up the receiver. 'Yes, sir,' they heard her say, 'everything is quite all right. I can manage the children, even if they do make things a bit difficult. Don't you bother to come back until you're ready. I'll manage everything.'

George snatched the receiver out of Mrs Stick's hand.

'Hello, Father! It's me, George! How's Mother?'

'No worse, George,' said her father. 'I'm glad to hear from Mrs Stick that everything is all right. I'm very worried, and I'm glad to feel that I can tell your mother that everything is going smoothly at Kirrin Cottage.'

'But it *isn't*!' said George wildly. 'It's all horrid. Can't the Sticks go and let us manage things by ourselves?'

'Good gracious me, of course not,' said her father, sounding annoyed. 'I did hope, George, that you would be sensible and helpful. I must say . . .'

'*You* talk to him, Julian,' said George helplessly, and she thrust the receiver into Julian's hand.

Go to **89**.

81

If you've arrived from **76**, *score* ◁.

Julian looked around the room. He suddenly saw a letter addressed to George stuck in the rim of the big mirror. He gave it to her. It was from her father.

George read the letter out loud.

Dear George,

Your mother has been taken very ill. I'm going with her to the hospital and will stay with her until she's feeling better. That may be in a few days' time, or in a week's time. I'll telephone you each day at nine o'clock in the morning to tell you how she is. Mrs Stick will look after you all. Try to manage all right until I come back.

Your loving Father

George's eyes filled with tears. 'I can't bear Mother going away like this!' she sobbed, and buried her head in the cushions.

Go to **65**.

82

George rushed into the house and picked up the telephone.

'Hello, hello, is that you, Father?' she said. 'Oh, hello, Aunt Jane! Did you want to speak to Julian?' She turned to Julian, who was standing beside her. 'It's your mother,' she hissed. 'Don't tell her that my mother is in hospital, or she'll say that you all have to go home, and I'll be left on my own with those Sticks!'

Julian took the receiver.

'Hello, Mother!' he said. 'How are you and Father?'

'We're very well,' replied his mother. 'And how are all of you? Not being a nuisance to Fanny and Quentin, I hope?'

Julian winked at the others.

'Oh, no, Mother,' he replied. 'We're definitely not being a nuisance to Aunt Fanny and Uncle Quentin!'

Dick grinned. He knew that Julian was thinking that he hadn't told a lie, because Aunt Fanny and Uncle Quentin weren't there to be annoyed!

'By the way,' went on the children's mother, 'why did George think I might be her father? Isn't he there?'

Go to **88.**

83

'Don't be silly,' said Julian. 'We all stand together in this. If you've got a plan, we'll come into it, but we're staying here with you whatever happens.'

George looked ashamed.

'Sorry!' she said. 'I'm an idiot. I won't argue with you. Now, what shall we do today?'

It wasn't a happy day. Mrs Stick refused to make them a picnic lunch, so they had to buy sausage rolls in the village. George didn't want to be too far from the house in case her father phoned, so they all messed about, doing nothing very much.

At teatime Mrs Stick provided them with bread and butter and jam, but no cake. The milk was sour too, and everyone had to have tea without milk, which they all disliked.

As they ate their tea, the children heard Edgar outside the window. In his hand he held a tin bowl, which he put down on the grass outside.

'Your dog's dinner!' he yelled.

George had got up to see if there were any biscuits on the sideboard. As she turned her back, Timmy slipped out of the room. George just caught sight of his tail disappearing through the door.

'Timmy!' she shouted. 'Come back! Don't touch that meat!' She rushed after the dog.

If you think George manages to get to the bowl before Timmy does, go to **91**.
If you think Timmy reaches the bowl first, go to **97**.

84

No supper appeared that evening, so Julian took Timmy and went along to the kitchen.

'What do you want?' asked Mrs Stick, turning off the radio.

'Supper, please, Mrs Stick,' said Julian. He walked past her and opened the larder door.

'Oh, good, a chicken – and some tomatoes!' exclaimed the boy. 'And a *wonderful* treacle tart – how delicious!'

'That's *our* supper,' said Mrs Stick. 'Here – you can have bread and cheese.' She looked at him as if to say, 'Do as I tell you, or you'll find yourself in big trouble . . .'

Julian hesitated.

If you think he should take the bread and cheese, go to **93**.
If not, go to **100**.

85

If you've arrived from **77**, *score* ◯⌐.

Julian went back to the others with a gloomy face.

'She's locked the door,' he said. 'She really is a dreadful creature. I don't believe we'll get any supper tonight.'

'We'll have to wait until she goes to bed,' said George. 'We'll go down and hunt in the larder then, and see what we can find.'

They went to bed hungry. Julian listened for Mrs Stick and Edgar to go to bed too. When he had heard them come upstairs, and was sure their doors were shut, he slipped down to the kitchen. It was dark there, and Julian was just about to put on the light when he heard the sound of someone breathing heavily. Was it Stinker? But it sounded like a human being.

He snapped on the light.

If you think Julian sees somebody when he turns on the light, go to **79**.
If not, go to **90**.

George reached the phone first and grabbed the receiver. 'Hello! This is Kirrin 246. Is that you, Father?'

'Hello, George,' said her father. 'Is Mrs Stick there? I'd like to speak to her, please.'

'Oh, but Father!' exclaimed George. 'There are several things I want to tell you, and I want to know how Mother is!'

'First let me speak to Mrs Stick,' her father replied. 'I'll talk to you after I've spoken to her. Now please find her and tell her I'd like to speak to her.'

'She's right here,' said George, putting the receiver down on the table. 'My father wants to speak to you, Mrs Stick,' she said crossly, turning to the housekeeper.

Go to **80.**

87

George walked into the kitchen, where Mrs Stick was making pastry.

'What do you mean by trying to feed my dog rotten meat?' she demanded angrily. 'Look at the maggots in this!' She thrust the bowl under Mrs Stick's nose.

'Those aren't maggots,' said Mrs Stick. 'Those are just bits of fat in the meat, that's all.'

'They're maggots!' George shouted. She walked

over to the rubbish bin and threw the meat into it.

'Here, don't you go wasting good meat like that, my girl,' said Mrs Stick. 'There was nothing wrong with that – just a few bits of fat in it!'

'In future just leave my dog alone,' said George. 'Don't try to feed him *anything*!' She went back to the others.

Go to **102**.

88

'Oh . . . er . . . Uncle Quentin isn't here just at this moment,' said Julian. 'He's gone out. We thought he might be ringing up to say that he won't be back for supper. Would you like a word with Anne or Dick?'

Dick and Anne both spoke to their mother, and then the children went back into the garden.

'That was a bit difficult!' said Dick. 'I'm quite sure that if our parents knew that Aunt Fanny was in hospital they would insist that we went home at once!'

'I hope they don't ring again, and speak to Mrs Stick,' said Anne. 'I'm sure she'd say that she didn't want us here.'

'Mother didn't say anything about ringing again,' said Julian. 'I shouldn't worry about that.'

Just then the telephone rang a second time.

Go to **74**.

'Well, Uncle Quentin,' began Julian, wondering how he would explain to his quick-tempered uncle what was happening at Kirrin Cottage, 'I must tell you that . . .'

There was a click on the other end of the telephone. Uncle Quentin had gone. 'Blow!' said Julian. 'He cut me off.'

'Serves you right!' called Mrs Stick as she went back into the kitchen. 'Now you'll all have to behave yourselves, or it'll be the worse for you.' She slammed the door behind her.

'You three had better go back home,' said George suddenly. 'I've got a plan of my own, and you're not in it. Ring your parents and go home tomorrow.'

Go to **83.**

The kitchen was flooded with radiance. Julian looked around. Everything seemed to be peaceful. The clock ticked briskly on the mantelpiece, and small noises came from the stove as the coal shifted, but that was all. Julian hesitated. He was sure he'd heard the noise of someone breathing, but there wasn't anyone there! It was very odd.

Leaving the light on, he moved towards the larder door and opened it. There was enough light from the kitchen for him to see what was on the shelves, and he spotted what looked like a meat pie and, further along, some jam tarts. They would be just right for four hungry children.

But all of a sudden somebody coughed in the kitchen.

Go to **75.**

91

George dashed past Timmy and grabbed the bowl just as the dog reached it. She picked it up and inspected the meat.

'This meat's rotten!' she said in disgust. 'I can see maggots in it. You would have been awfully ill if you'd eaten this, Timmy.'

Dick leaned out of the window.

'I think it's beastly of Mrs Stick to try to feed Timmy meat that would make him ill. How would she like it if we tried to feed Stinker rotten meat?' he said.

'I'm going to tell Mrs Stick exactly what I think of her rotten meat!' said George, and she marched off, carrying the bowl.

Go to **87.**

92

But George didn't seem to be carrying out any wild plan. She swam again with the others, went for a walk with them, and went rowing on the sea. She didn't want to go to Kirrin Island, so the others didn't press her, thinking that she didn't want to be out of sight of the beach in case Edgar came with a message from her father.

It was quite a pleasant day. The children bought sausage rolls and fruit again, and picnicked on the beach. Timmy had a large and juicy bone from the butcher.

'I've got a bit of shopping to do,' said George at about teatime. 'Why don't you others go and see if Mrs Stick is getting some tea for us.'

'I'll come with you,' said Julian, getting up. 'Dick can tackle Mrs Stick for once.'

'Oh, no, I can't,' said Dick. 'Anyway, I want to buy a couple of postcards.'

'That means Anne will have to come too,' said Julian. 'She can't go back to the Sticks by herself.'

George glared at them all. 'I want to go on my own,' she said. 'You three go home, *please*!'

If you think they all go shopping, go to **96.**
If you think George goes on her own, go to **101.**

93

His eyes gleaming with mischief, Julian said: 'All right, Mrs Stick, I'll take the bread and cheese.'

Mrs Stick bustled around the kitchen, getting a loaf of bread from the big breadbin, and cheese and butter from the fridge. She piled it all on to a tray with some plates and knives.

'There you are,' she said. 'Now, off you go and leave us to have our supper in peace!'

'There are one or two other things I'd like to take,' said Julian, and he fetched the chicken, tomatoes and treacle tart out of the larder and put them on the tray.

'Here – what do you think you're doing?' shouted Mrs Stick. 'Put those back!'

Go to **105.**

94

If you've arrived from **103**, *score* ◯ᴘ.

Julian read the note through.

'Why didn't I *guess* that was her plan!' he said to himself. 'That's why we didn't come into it. She meant to go off by herself with Timmy. I can't let her do that. She can't live all by herself on Kirrin Island for so long. She might fall ill. She might slip on a rock and hurt herself, and no one would ever know!'

He wondered what to do. That noise he had heard must have been made by George. So she couldn't have had a very long start. If he tore down to the beach George might still be there, and he could stop her. Or should he wake Dick and Anne first, and tell them? He didn't like the idea of them waking up to find him gone.

If you think he should hurry after George, go to **108.**
If you think he should first warn Dick and Anne, go to **116.**

Julian stopped and listened hard. Somebody was running along the beach. He turned around and shone his torch in front of him. There were George and Timmy!

'George!' he called. 'Where have you been? I was getting worried about you!'

George scowled at him. 'Timmy saw a rabbit and chased off after it,' she explained. 'I had to go and get him. You know what he's like about rabbits. But what are you doing here, Julian?'

'I wanted to tell you not to go off to Kirrin Island on your own,' said Julian.

'You can't stop me!' retorted George.

'No, I can't,' said Julian. 'But listen, George! If you come back to Kirrin Cottage with me now, tomorrow we'll *all* go to Kirrin Island. Your mother said we could spend a week there, anyway, didn't she? We shall have a marvellous time!'

'Oh, Julian!' said George. 'What a very, very good idea!'

Go to **112.**

96

Julian was determined to go with George, however, because he was sure she was up to something, and, as Dick and Anne didn't want to face the

Sticks without Julian, they all went to the little general shop in the village.

George bought a new battery for her torch, two boxes of matches and a bottle of methylated spirits.

'Whatever do you want that for?' asked Anne in surprise.

'Oh, it might come in useful,' replied George, and said no more.

Go to **104.**

97

But when Timmy got to the bowl he just sniffed at it, then pushed the bowl with his nose. George came dashing out. She picked up the bowl and looked at the meat.

'This meat's rotten!' she said in disgust. 'I can see maggots in it. You didn't touch it, did you, Timmy? It would make you awfully ill if you ate it.'

Dick leaned out of the window.

'No, he didn't eat any. I watched him. He sniffed all around it, but he wouldn't touch it.'

George was very white.

'Oh, Timmy!' she said. 'You're such a sensible dog. You wouldn't touch rotten meat, would you?'

Timmy wagged his tail.

Go to **102.**

Julian's torch picked out a white envelope pinned to George's pillow. It had his name written on it. He picked it up, ripped it open and read it:

Dear Julian,

Don't be angry with me, please. I daren't stay in Kirrin Cottage any longer in case the Sticks somehow poison Timmy. So I've gone to live by myself on our island until Mother and Father come back. Please leave a note for Father and tell him to ask Jim to sail near Kirrin Island with his red flag flying from the mast as soon as they are back. Then I'll come home. You and Dick and Anne must go back to your parents now I've gone. It would be silly to stay at Kirrin Cottage with the Sticks now I'm not there.

Love from George

Go to **94.**

If you've arrived from **111**, *score* ◯↰.

The boat was still sitting on the beach, but Julian couldn't see George. He flashed his torch all around the boat, and inside it, but she was no-where to be found. Julian sat down on the sand for a moment, completely baffled. Where on earth could she have gone?

She couldn't have gone back to Kirrin Cottage, because he would have met her on the road. But where could she be, in the middle of the night? It was all very odd, and Julian began to get worried.

Finally he stood up. He would have to go back to Kirrin Cottage and tell the others that he couldn't find George, and then they could all decide what to do.

But just as he was setting off back along the beach, he thought he heard a noise.

Go to **95.**

100

'Oh, no, Mrs Stick,' said Julian. '*You* can have bread and cheese!'

He picked up the chicken and balanced the tart on top of it. He could just manage the tomatoes,

too. As he started towards the kitchen door, Mrs Stick made an angry noise and went after him with her hand raised. But Timmy immediately leapt at her, and his teeth snapped together with a loud click.

Mrs Stick took a step backwards. 'You keep that dog away from me!' she exclaimed.

'With pleasure!' retorted Julian, and he marched triumphantly out of the kitchen.

Go to **110.**

101

Julian looked at George for a moment. It was obvious that she was up to something, but he didn't want to upset her by insisting that he went to the shop with her. Poor George had enough to worry about at the moment, with her mother in hospital.

'All right, George,' he said. 'You go and do your shopping, and we'll see you back at Kirrin Cottage.'

George grinned. 'Thanks, Julian,' she said, and walked off towards the village.

'Come on, you two,' said Julian to the others. 'We'll go back and see if Mrs Stick has some tea for us.'

Go to **109.**

*If you've arrived from **87**, score ⌢.*

After tea George still looked rather upset.

'Cheer up,' said Julian. 'Timmy's fine.'

'Yes, but I can't help thinking that if the Sticks tried to give him rotten meat, and that didn't work, they might try to give him poisoned meat next time!' said George.

'They wouldn't do that,' said Julian. 'You're getting into a fuss over nothing. People can't go around poisoning dogs when they feel like it! It's against the law, for a start.'

'I don't think that would bother the Sticks,' muttered George, but she said no more.

*Go to **84**.*

Julian shone his torch on the bedside table, noticing as he did so that George's torch and watch were missing, then flashed the beam along the mantelpiece. There it was – a' white envelope with his name on it. He picked it up and read the note:

Dear Julian,

Don't be angry with me, please. I daren't stay in Kirrin Cottage any longer in case the Sticks somehow poison Timmy. So I've gone to live by myself on our island until Mother and Father come back. Please leave a note for Father and tell him to ask Jim to sail near Kirrin Island with his red flag flying from the mast as soon as they are back. Then I'll come home. You and Dick and Anne must go back to your parents now I've gone. It would be silly to stay at Kirrin Cottage with the Sticks now I'm not there.

Love from George

Go to **94.**

104

If you've arrived from **109**, *score* ◯⌐.

After tea, as it was raining, the children played cards. When suppertime came, Mrs Stick provided cold ham, cheese and the remains of a milk pudding. There was also a plate of cooked meat for Timmy.

George looked at it sharply. 'Take that away!' she said, 'I wouldn't be surprised if you've poisoned it. Take it away!'

'On the contrary,' said Julian, 'leave it here. I'll take it down to the chemist's tomorrow and get him to test it. If, as George thinks, it's poisoned, the chemist might have a lot of interesting things to tell us.'

Mrs Stick took the meat away without a word.

'Horrible woman!' said George, pulling Timmy close to her. 'How I dislike her! I'm so afraid for Timmy.'

By ten o'clock they were all very sleepy. They had swum, walked and rowed that day, and were tired. Julian tried to stay awake for a little while, but he too fell asleep very quickly.

Later in the night he awoke with a jump, thinking he had heard a noise. But everything was quiet. What could the noise have been?

I suppose it's not old George doing anything about that plan of hers! thought Julian suddenly. He sat up and felt around for his dressing-gown. Putting it on, he crept into the girls' room and switched on his torch to see that they were all right.

Anne was sleeping peacefully, but George's bed was empty!

Go to **113**.

105

Julian shook his head.

'Oh, no, Mrs Stick,' he said. 'You offered me bread and cheese, so I thought I might as well take it. After all, we're all very hungry. But I want the chicken and the other things as well.'

Mrs Stick made an angry noise and started to go after Julian with her hand raised. But Timmy immediately leapt at her, and his teeth snapped together with a loud click.

Mrs Stick took a step backwards. 'Keep that dog away from me!' she said. 'And what do you suppose we're going to have for *our* supper?'

'Bread and cheese, Mrs Stick,' said Julian. 'There's plenty more bread in the bin, and lots of cheese in the fridge!'

He marched triumphantly out of the kitchen.

Go to **110**.

106

Julian swept his torch around the room, looking for anything that might be a note from George. He had to be very careful not to wake up Anne, who would be upset when she saw that George wasn't in bed. First of all he looked on George's pillow, thinking that was the most obvious place, but there was nothing there. Then he looked under the pillow, even though he didn't think it was very likely that George would have left a note there. There was nothing under the pillow except George's untidily folded pyjamas.

'She must have planned to leave the house,' said Julian to himself. 'She wouldn't have bothered to get dressed if she'd just gone downstairs or to the bathroom or something. She *must* have left a note, but where is it?'

Go to **103.**

107

They raced up the stairs and into their own rooms. Luckily Tinker was barking very loudly now, and the noise he made covered the sound of their feet on the stairs.

The bedroom door had just closed behind Dick, who had been last up the stairs, when the door of Mrs Stick's room opened and she came out on to the landing. She opened the door of George and Anne's bedroom, and flashed her torch inside. There was a head on each pillow, and the sound of even breathing. It was the same in the boys' room.

'Well, I don't know what Tinker heard to make him bark like that,' Mrs Stick said to herself. 'It was probably that dratted dog of George's.'

She went back to bed.

Go to **114.**

108

Julian decided to go after George. With any luck he could catch up with her and stop her. Still in his dressing-gown, he slipped downstairs and out of the front door, and ran down the road to the beach.

He hurried along the beach towards the place where George kept her boat, and flashed his torch in front of him. Would the boat still be on the beach, or had George already gone?

If you think the boat is still there, go to **99.**
If you think the boat has gone, go to **120.**

109

George went to the little general shop in the village, which sold almost everything from shoelaces to saucepans. She bought a bottle of methylated spirits, a new battery for her torch and some matches.

'Going camping, George?' asked Mrs Jenks, behind the counter.

'No,' said George. 'These are just a few things that I thought we were short of at home.'

'And how is your mother now?' went on Mrs Jenks.

'Oh, she's getting better, thank you,' replied George. 'She should be home in about ten days.'

'I'm very pleased to hear that,' said Mrs Jenks. 'Do give her my best wishes, won't you?'

'I'll do that,' said George. 'Thanks, Mrs Jenks. Goodbye!'

She set off back to Kirrin Cottage.

Go to **104.**

110

If you've arrived from **105**, *score* ◯◁.

The children had a very good supper and went to bed soon afterwards. They were up early the next morning and went for a swim before breakfast. It was a marvellous day, the sky clear and blue and the sea smooth and calm.

Uncle Quentin telephoned after breakfast. He told George that her mother had had an operation the previous day, and that they would both be home in about ten days. George was overjoyed that her mother was going to be all right, and she ate an enormous breakfast, reluctantly provided by Mrs Stick. Then George said something that made Julian cross.

'Well, now that I know that Mother is getting better, I can stand up to the Sticks all right by myself with Timmy. So I want you three to go back home and finish the hols without me. I shall be all right.'

'Stop it, George,' said Julian. 'We're not going home and leaving you on your own!'

'I told you I've got a plan,' said George, 'and you don't come into it, I'm afraid. You'll find you have to go home whether you mean to or not.'

She wouldn't say another word. Julian secretly made up his mind not to let George out of his sight that day. If she were going to carry out some wild plan, then she would have to do it under his eye!

Go to **92.**

111

Julian gave the note to Dick.

'Goodness,' said Dick. 'She might have asked us to go too! We were going to spend a week on Kirrin Island anyway, weren't we?'

'I'm going to go after George,' said Julian. 'I'm going to persuade her that we should all go and live on the island until her parents come home. You two stay here, and I'll be as quick as I can.'

Julian left Dick and Anne talking in excited whispers and slipped down the stairs as quietly as he could. Still in his dressing-gown, he let himself out of the front door and ran down the road to the beach.

He walked along the beach towards the place where George kept her boat, and flashed his torch in front of him. Would the boat still be on the beach, or had George already gone?

If you think the boat is still there, go to **99.**
If you think the boat has gone, go to **120.**

112

If you've arrived from **95**, *score* ⌒⌐.

Julian and George made their way back to the house, feeling excited. Dick and Anne were waiting for them, and they all discussed their plans in whispers. The main problem was getting enough food, until George remembered that in her mother's bedroom was a store-cupboard in which she kept plenty of tinned food in case Kirrin Cottage was cut off from the village by snow, which happened sometimes.

As quietly as they could, they collected food from the larder and store-cupboard, water, blankets, pillows, and all the other things they thought they might need on the island. They piled it into a heap in the kitchen.

Anne looked at it.

'How are we going to get all this down to George's boat?' she asked. 'We'll never be able to carry it all!'

'We could load it all into a wheelbarrow,' suggested Julian. 'There's one in the garden shed. We can wheel it down the sandy side of the road so that it won't make a noise.'

'Oh, good idea,' said George. 'The wheelbarrow

has a squeaky wheel, but we'll hope no one hears it.'

But Tinker heard the squeak as he lay in a corner of Mrs Stick's room. He lifted one ear, and a low noise started at the back of his throat.

If you think Tinker growls, go to **122**.
If not, go to **117**.

113

George's clothes were missing, too.

'Blow!' said Julian under his breath. 'Where has she gone? I bet she's run away to find where her mother is! I wonder if she's left a note anywhere?'

Just then Anne turned over and muttered something. Julian switched off his torch so as not to wake her and stood in the dark, thinking hard. Surely George wouldn't have just walked out of the house without leaving a message for them all.

'I bet she's left a note somewhere,' Julian said to himself. 'But *where*?'

Turning on his torch again, he began to look around the room.

If you think he finds a note on George's pillow, go to **98**.
If not, go to **106**.

114

If you've arrived from **121**, *score* ◁.

Julian counted to a thousand to give Mrs Stick time to go to sleep again, then he got up. 'Dick!' he said quietly. 'Are you awake?'

'Of course I am,' said Dick.

The two boys collected George and Anne from their room, and soon they were wheeling the wheelbarrow down the road to the boat. After everything had been neatly stowed on board it was still too dark to set off for the island. The children didn't like the idea of leaving all the provisions unguarded while they went back to the house, and in the end they decided to leave Dick there, sleeping on the rugs.

'Right,' said Julian. 'Come on, you two. Goodbye, Dick. We'll be down very early to row off.'

The three of them set off back to the house with Timmy.

Go to **119.**

115

'We'll call on Alf before we go, then,' said Julian. 'Now, let's look for that timetable.'

They hunted for the timetable, found the right place, and underlined the train they hoped the Sticks would think they were catching.

'Right,' said Julian. 'Now we'll creep upstairs and make a lot of noise as if we were just getting up. Come on.'

The three children and Timmy went up to their rooms, and George whistled to Timmy, while Julian sang at the top of his voice. Then, with a great banging of doors, they set out down the path and cut across the moors, in full sight of the kitchen window.

'Hope the Sticks won't notice that Dick isn't with us,' said Julian, seeing Edgar staring out of the kitchen window. 'I expect they'll think he's gone on ahead.'

They kept to the path until they came to a dip, where they were hidden from any watcher at Kirrin Cottage, then they doubled back down another path to where they had left Dick in the boat.

'Ahoy there!' yelled Julian in excitement. 'Dick!'

They expected to see Dick standing beside the boat, but there was no sign of him.

'Maybe he's still asleep,' suggested Anne.

'Surely Julian's shouting would have woken him,' said George.

If you think Dick is in the boat, go to **124.**
If not, go to **132.**

116

After a moment's thought Julian decided to wake Dick and Anne. Goodness knows what they might think if they were to find that both he and George had vanished.

'Anne! Anne!' he whispered, giving his sister's shoulder a gentle shake.

Anne stirred and slowly opened her eyes.

'W . . . what is it, Julian?' she said drowsily. 'Surely it isn't time to get up yet, is it? I don't feel as if I've been asleep very long.'

'No,' Julian hissed. 'It's still the middle of the

night. But George has gone! Here – read this note she left while I go and wake Dick.'

Anne sat up and turned on the bedside light. While she was reading George's note Julian re-appeared, followed by a sleepy Dick.

'What's happening?' said Dick. 'Where's George?'

Go to **111.**

117

All of a sudden, Tinker jumped up and gave three loud barks.

Mrs Stick sat up in bed. 'What is it?' she said. 'What's the matter, Tinker?'

Tinker barked again. Mrs Stick turned on the light.

'Half-past three!' she said, looking at her clock. 'There must be something going on if Tinker's barking. I'd better go and take a look.'

Downstairs, the children had been about to load the wheelbarrow when they heard Tinker barking.

'Oh, no!' Dick had groaned. 'That dog will wake Mrs Stick, and then we'll be in trouble.'

Mrs Stick's room was over the kitchen, and they heard the floor creak as she got out of bed.

'She's getting up!' hissed George.

'Come on,' said Julian. 'Back to bed – and pretend you're sound asleep!'

If you think they get back to their rooms without Mrs Stick seeing them, go to **107.**
If you think she sees any of them, go to **125.**

If you've arrived from **128**, *score* ◯↰.

The sea was fairly calm, but a good breeze blew
through their hair. The water splashed around the
boat and made a gurgly, friendly noise. The
children all felt very happy. They were on their
own. They were escaping from the horrid Sticks.
They were going to stay on Kirrin Island with the
rabbits and gulls and jackdaws.

'I don't believe anyone noticed us going,' said
Julian. 'Except Alf, of course.'

They had called at Alf's house on their way to
the boat, and he had promised to let them know
when George's father and mother came back.

Go to **130**.

If you've arrived from **114**, *score* ◁ ◁.

George, Julian and Anne talked about what to tell the Sticks.

'I think we won't tell them anything,' said Julian at last. 'I know what we'll do – there's a train that leaves the station at about eight o'clock, which would be the one we'd catch if we were going back to our own home. We'll find a timetable, leave it open on the dining-room table as if we've been looking up a train, and then we'll set off across the moor at the back of the house, as if we were going to the station.'

'That's a good idea,' said George, pleased. 'But how shall we know when Father and Mother get back?'

'Is there anyone you could leave a message with – someone you can trust?' asked Julian.

George thought hard. 'There's Alf, who's the son of a fisherman. He used to look after Timmy for me when I wasn't allowed to have him in the house. I know he wouldn't give us away.'

Go to **115**.

If you've arrived from **111**, *score* ◁.

The boat was not on the beach. Julian heard the splash of oars and ran down to the water's edge.

Shining his torch in front of him, he could see George sitting in her boat a short distance from the shore. Timmy was with her.

'George! Idiot!' he called. 'You're not to go off all alone like this, in the dead of night!'

'You can't stop me!' George called back.

Julian waded out to the boat and climbed in.

'Listen!' he said. 'If you come back to Kirrin Cottage with me now, tomorrow we'll *all* go to Kirrin Island. Your mother said we could spend a week there, anyway, didn't she? We shall have a marvellous time!'

'Oh, Julian!' said George. 'What a very, very good idea!'

Go to **112.**

121

'And why are you hiding a packet of biscuits behind your back?' went on Mrs Stick, staring at Dick, who had been about to put the biscuits in the wheelbarrow when they'd had to dash upstairs.

Julian had a sudden idea. 'We were going to have a midnight feast,' he said. 'You didn't give us much supper, and we were hungry, so we decided to find some food in the kitchen and have a feast in our bedroom.'

'But why are you dressed?' said Mrs Stick. 'You wouldn't need to get dressed just to go down to the kitchen.'

'It's very cold,' said Julian. 'We thought we'd be more comfortable like this.'

It wasn't cold at all, it was a warm summer night, but Julian hoped that Mrs Stick wouldn't think of that!

'Well, you'd better get back to bed,' she said. 'Give me them biscuits. Midnight feasts, indeed!'

She went back to her room.

Julian turned to Dick. 'Let's go and lie down in our beds and pretend to be asleep, just in case she comes to check on us. We'd better wait a while before we get up again.'

Go to **114.**

122

The low noise became a deep growl, and Mrs Stick stirred in her sleep. Tinker stopped growling and listened. The house was silent. Mrs Stick rolled over and went on sleeping.

After everything had been stowed into the boat, it was still too dark to set off for the island. The children didn't like the idea of leaving all the provisions unguarded while they went back to the house, and in the end they decided to leave Dick there, sleeping on the rugs.

'I hope we've remembered all we shall want,' said George. 'Golly – I know! We forgot about a tin-opener!'

'We can pick one up at the house,' said Julian. 'Come on, you two. Goodbye, Dick. We'll be down very early to row off.'

The three of them set off back to the house with Timmy.

Go to **119.**

*If you've arrived from **142**, score* ◁ ◁.

George insisted on taking the oars, however, and the others watched in admiration as she guided the boat skilfully in and out of the hidden rocks. They they slid into the little cove. It was a natural harbour, with the water running up to a stretch of sand. High rocks sheltered it. The children jumped out eagerly, and four pairs of willing hands tugged the boat quickly up the sand.

'Higher up still,' panted George. 'You know what awful storms suddenly blow up in this bay. We want to be sure the boat is safe, no matter how rough the seas are.'

Go to **127**.

124

Julian peered into the boat and began to laugh. 'He's here, all right,' he said. 'Look!'

Dick was curled up under several blankets right at the bottom of the boat, with just the top of his head sticking out. He was sound asleep.

'Come on, Dick!' said George. 'Wake up! Our adventure is about to begin.'

Dick yawned and stretched.

'Oh, hello!' he said. 'Is it time to go?'

'It is,' said Julian. 'Up you get.'

The other three children and Timmy clambered

into the boat. Timmy ran up to the prow, where he always stood.

'Off we go!' said Julian, taking the oars. 'Sit over there a bit, Anne. The luggage is weighing the boat down at the other end. Dick, could you sit by Anne to keep the balance right?'

Off they went in George's boat, rocking up and down on the waves.

Go to **118.**

125

They raced up the stairs. Anne and George made it into their room and jumped into bed, but Julian and Dick weren't so lucky. Julian had his hand on the door of their room when Mrs Stick came out on to the landing.

Dick tried not to laugh, even though he was feeling a bit scared. Mrs Stick looked so awful, with her hair in rollers and wearing an ugly old camel-coloured dressing-gown. She looked a perfect fright!

'Here, what are you boys doing, running about the house in the middle of the night, disturbing folk's sleep?' she demanded. 'And why have you got your clothes on?'

Julian and Dick looked at each other. Neither of them could think what to say!

Go to **121.**

All four reached the rocks and pulled themselves out of the water. The rocks were jagged and sharp, and the children had to be careful how they moved about on them. They sat in a row, enjoying the sun and the slight breeze that blew off the sea.

'I'm hungry,' said Dick after a while.

'You're always hungry!' retorted George. 'I'm going to climb up on that big rock and do some diving before we swim back to the beach.'

'Won't that be dangerous?' asked Julian. 'After all, you should never dive without knowing what might be under the water. There could be some very sharp rocks down there.'

'It's all right, Julian,' said George. 'I've been diving off that rock for years – there's good deep water under it.'

'I think we should go back and have lunch,' said Dick. 'You can come and dive another day, George. After all, we're going to be here a week, at least!'

If you think George should go diving, go to **143.**
If you think they should go back to the beach for lunch, go to **135.**

If you've arrived from **133**, *score* ◯ ◯ ◯.

The boat soon lay on one side, high up on the stretch of sand. The children sat down, puffing and blowing. 'Let's have breakfast here,' said Julian. 'I don't feel like unloading all those heavy things at the moment. We'll get what we want for breakfast and have it here on this warm patch of sand.'

The children had a large breakfast, as they were very hungry. After they'd eaten they all began to feel very sleepy. One by one they dropped off to sleep on the warm sand. Timmy lay down beside George, put his head right on her middle and closed his eyes.

Go to **139**.

128

The three of them sat down beside the boat and waited for Dick. After two or three minutes he suddenly appeared from behind the sand-dunes at the back of the beach.

'Hello!' he said. 'All ready to go?'

'Where have you been, Dick?' asked George. 'We were beginning to get a bit worried about you.'

'I went off to see if I could find some sticks,' said Dick, holding up a handful of wood. 'I was getting very cold waiting for you, and I thought I'd light a little fire.'

'Well, there's no need for you to do that now,' said Julian. 'We're off on our adventure!'

The children climbed into the boat, and Timmy ran up to his usual position in the prow.

'Off we go!' said Julian, taking the oars. 'Sit over there a bit, Anne. The luggage is weighing the boat down at the other end. Dick, could you sit by Anne to keep the balance right?'

Off they went in George's boat, rocking up and down on the waves.

Go to **118.**

129

None of them really liked the idea of sleeping in the dungeons, so they decided to go and look at the wreck.

'I don't somehow fancy living on a damp old rotting wreck,' said Julian, 'but maybe the sun will have dried it enough for us to have our stores and beds there.'

'Let's go and see,' said George.

They made their way from the ruined castle to the old wall that ran around it. From there they would be able to see the wreck. It had been cast up the year before, after lying for many years under the water, and it had settled firmly on the rocks.

Go to **134.**

Dick turned and faced the island. 'We shall soon be there,' he said. 'Hadn't you better let George take the oars and guide the boat into the inlet, Julian?'

'I think I'd better,' said George. 'You know how tricky that inlet can be.'

'Well, I'd like to try it, George,' replied Julian. 'After all, I can row nearly as well as you now, and it would be a good idea if more than one of us knew how to get the boat into the inlet.'

'I know you can row pretty well,' said George, 'but the boat is very heavily laden at the moment and may be difficult to control, so I think I'd better do it.'

'I *would* like to try it,' repeated Julian.

If you think George should take the oars, go to **123.**
If you think Julian should keep them, go to **136.**

'Oh, yes, Julian, let's go for a swim,' begged Anne. 'I'm *so* hot!'

'All right,' said Julian. 'But we mustn't be too long.'

The children dug their swimming costumes out of the heap of clothes in the boat, and changed quickly. The water felt cool and refreshing.

'Let's swim over to the rocks,' said George, pointing to the jagged rocks that jutted out into the sea. Wedged on the rocks was the wreck – a big old sailing-ship that had once been captained by one of George's ancestors.

Julian and George were very strong swimmers, and Dick was nearly as good. Anne was not as good as the other three, but she'd been having lessons in the school pool and could swim much better than she'd been able to the year before.

Go to **126.**

132

But when they got to the boat, there was no sign of Dick.

'Where on earth can he be?' said Julian. 'He was supposed to be guarding all our stuff. It's not like him to have wandered off and left it.'

'Perhaps he's gone for an early-morning swim,' suggested Anne.

'I suppose he might have done,' said Julian doubtfully.

They stared along the beach. There was no one in sight at all, just gulls swooping over the sea.

'He can't possibly have gone to visit anyone,' said George. 'It's much too early for that!'

'Perhaps he thought of something that we might have forgotten, and he went back to Kirrin Cottage to get it. We came down a different path this time, so we wouldn't have seen him,' suggested Anne.

'Well, wherever he's gone we'll just have to sit and wait until he comes back,' said Julian. 'I hope he's not too long. We don't want anyone asking us what we're doing!'

Go to **128.**

133

George watched as Julian rowed as far as he could before her three cousins got out of the boat and started to pull it up the sand. She didn't think they had pulled it up high enough to be safe from the storms that could blow up so suddenly in the bay, but she was determined not to say anything.

Julian looked over to where George was sitting and felt very sorry for her. She had been quite right – it had been difficult for him to get the boat into the inlet – and, besides, she hadn't had a very good time over the past few days, worrying about her mother. He walked over to her.

'I'm sorry, George,' he said. 'You were quite right about the boat. Don't be cross any more.'

George got up and smiled at him. It was nice of him to apologise, and she stopped feeling cross.

'That's all right,' she said. 'But we'd better get the boat higher up the beach, to be on the safe side.'

Go to **127.**

They stood on the wall and looked at the wreck, but it wasn't where they had expected it.

'It's moved,' said Julian in surprise. 'There it is – on those rocks – nearer to the shore than it was before. Poor old wreck! It's been battered about a good bit over the winter, hasn't it? It looks much more of a real wreck than it did last summer.'

'I don't believe we shall be able to sleep there,' said Dick. 'It's dreadfully battered. We might be able to store food there, though. Do you know, I believe we could get to it from those rocks that run out from the island.'

'Yes, I believe we could,' said George. 'We could only reach it safely by boat last summer, couldn't we? But when the tide is low I think we *could* climb over the line of rocks right to the wreck itself.'

'We'll try later,' said Julian. 'Now we really must decide where we're going to sleep.'

'Where shall we look?' asked Anne.

Go to **146.**

George hesitated. She loved diving, but she was hungry too.

'All right, then,' she said. 'We'll go back and have lunch. You're quite right, Dick. I can always come and dive tomorrow.'

They swam back to where they'd left the boat

and were soon sitting on the beach eating large
sandwiches and drinking ginger beer and lemonade. George had brought a bone for Timmy, and
some of his special biscuits. He found a little pool of
rainwater among the rocks and drank out of that.

'What shall we do next?' asked Anne.

Go to **147.**

136

George looked at Julian for a moment.

'All right,' she said. 'You can try it, but you'll
have to give the oars to me if you get into trouble.'

Julian began to guide the boat in and out of the
hidden rocks. The other three watched him anxiously. Julian could row quite well, but the entrance to the little inlet on Kirrin Island where they
always left the boat was rather tricky to reach.

Julian was finding it very difficult to row and
manoeuvre the boat around the rocks at the same
time. The boat began drifting sideways, out to sea,
rather than in towards the island.

George couldn't bear it. 'Come on, Julian, give
me the oars!' she said.

'No,' panted Julian. 'I can manage!'

George got up and reached over to take the oars
from Julian, who refused to let go. The boat began
to swing wildly to and fro.

'Watch out!' shouted Dick. 'You'll have Timmy
in the water.'

Timmy, who was still standing in the prow, was

having trouble keeping his feet as the boat lurched.

If you think Timmy falls in, go to **142.**
If you think he manages to stay in the boat, go to **148.**

137

'George, you beast!' shouted Dick. 'You did frighten us. What *have* you found?'

George waded ashore.

'It's the top of the old figurehead that used to be on the front of the wreck,' she said. 'Most sailing-ships had figureheads, you know.'

'What, those funny things that look like women with no arms?' asked Anne.

'That's right,' said George. 'This must have fallen off the ship – probably when it was thrown up on the rocks by that storm last summer.'

Anne was still a bit pale.

'It looked horrible, with all the bits of seaweed hanging around it like hair,' she said. 'I half thought it was the ghost of a drowned person coming to haunt us!'

'I'm sorry if I frightened you, Anne,' said George. 'I'm going to take this head back home, I think, and maybe put it in my room, when it's had a chance to dry out.'

'We'd better be getting back to the island,' said Julian. 'There's still a lot to do. Come on!'

Soon they were back at the top of the inlet.

Go to **147.**

They stared at each other in amazement.

'Who did that?' asked George, frowning. '*We* didn't! Someone has been here!'

'Trippers, I suppose,' said Julian. 'Do you remember we thought we saw a spire of smoke here the other day? I bet it was trippers.'

'I think we should all have a good look around the castle to see if there are any more signs that people have been here,' said George.

'That's a good idea,' said Julian. 'I'll check the courtyard – you others search the rest of the castle.'

Anne and George went off to look around the jackdaw tower, while Dick went to the other, ruined tower. Suddenly they heard Julian shouting: 'Anne! George! Dick! Come here quickly!'

'Oh dear, perhaps he's hurt himself,' said Anne.

'Or maybe he's found something,' suggested George.

If you think Anne is right, go to **145**.
If you think George is right, go to **151**.

The sun was high in the sky before they woke up. Julian woke first, then Dick, who felt very hot with the sun blazing down.

Julian got to his feet. 'Wake up, George! Wake up, Anne!' he said. 'There's work to do!'

'Work to do! What do you mean?' asked George in astonishment.

'Well, we've got to unload the boat and pack everything away,' replied Julian, 'and decide where we're going to sleep.'

'Couldn't we go for a swim first?' suggested Dick. 'I'm terribly hot, and if we start taking stuff out of the boat we'll get even hotter. I'd love a swim to cool off.'

If you think they should go for a swim, go to **131.**
If you think they should unload the boat, go to **147.**

140

'I was walking across the courtyard when I caught my foot in something and fell,' said Julian rather stiffly.

Dick bent down and looked at the ground in front of the clump of brambles.

'That's what you caught your foot in,' he said, pointing to an iron ring attached to one of the stones of the courtyard floor. 'Now, let's see if we can get you out of there.'

It wasn't very easy pulling Julian out of the clump of brambles. His T-shirt and jeans were caught in several places, and his bare arms were badly scratched. At last they managed to untangle him, however, and he stood up, rubbing his arms.

George and Anne were still giggling from time to time, and Julian felt rather annoyed with them. Then suddenly he grinned. He probably *had* looked rather funny, stuck in a large clump of brambles!

'Come on,' he said. 'We'd better go on looking to see if anyone else has been here. Off you go!'

But they hadn't gone very far from the courtyard when they heard Julian calling again: 'Hey! I've found something!'

Go to **151.**

141

It was quite a shock to have their plans spoilt. They knew there was no other room in the ruined castle that was sufficiently whole to shelter them. And they had to find some sort of shelter, for although the weather was fine at the moment, it might rain hard any day – or a storm might blow up.

'We really must find some safe place and put our things there at once,' said Julian.

'But where shall we go?' asked Dick. 'There's no other place in the old castle.'

'There are the dungeons,' said Anne, shivering. 'But I don't think I want to sleep in one of them. It's so dark and mysterious down there.'

'Well, I suppose we could go and have a look,' said George. 'At least they'd give us a bit of shelter.'

'Or what about the wreck?' asked Dick. 'Shall we go and see if we could use that?'

If you think they should go and look at the wreck, go to **129.**

If you think they should check the dungeons, go to **146.**

142

The boat gave a violent roll, and with a startled *'Woof!'* Timmy fell into the water!

'Timmy!' shrieked George, abandoning her struggle for the oars and leaning over the side of the boat to try to grab the dog.

But Timmy was too far away for George to reach him. He knew that the children must be going to the island – they had been there so many times before – so he started to swim towards the shore. George watched him for a moment.

'He'll be all right,' she said. 'He'll get to the island before we do. Now, Julian, let me take the oars.'

'No, really,' said Julian. 'I'm sure I can manage.'

Go to **123.**

143

'You never think about anything but food, Dick!' scoffed George. 'You can surely wait a little longer for lunch, can't you?'

'I suppose so,' said Dick, sitting down on the rocks again.

George clambered up on to a tall rock nearby

and stood poised for a moment, her arms in front of her. Then she did a lovely clean dive into the water.

'My goodness, George is good at swimming and diving and rowing, isn't she?' said Anne. 'I'll never be as good as she is at any of those things.'

'Never mind,' said Julian, giving his sister a quick hug. 'There are lots of other things you can do well.'

Suddenly Anne gave a gasp and went quite white. 'Look!' she said, pointing at the sea. 'Look!'

Go to **150.**

144

'George! George!' shrieked Anne. 'Are you all right?'

George bobbed up beside the boat, spluttering and shaking her head.

'You silly idiot, Julian!' she shouted. 'You can jolly well try to get the boat into the inlet without my help now! I'm going to swim to the island. I'll see you there!' She began to swim strongly towards the island.

Julian set his lips in a determined line and started to row again. He found it a bit easier now that there was one less in the boat, and though it took him much longer than it would have taken George at last he managed to manoeuvre the boat up to the inlet.

George was sitting on the sand waiting for them, looking very sulky indeed.

Go to **133.**

145

Anne and George ran back to the courtyard, almost colliding with Dick, who came hurrying from the other side of the castle.

Julian was lying on his back in a large clump of brambles! He looked so comic that the other three started to laugh.

'I don't think it's funny,' said Julian. 'These brambles jolly well hurt! Come and help me get out of here!'

But the others were too overcome by laughter to help Julian straight away. Even Timmy was wagging his tail and grinning.

'W . . . what happened?' asked Dick, when he could speak. 'How on earth did you end up like that?'

Go to **140.**

146

If you've arrived from **134**, *score* ⌒⌒.

'I think we'd better go and inspect the dungeons,' said Julian, and they made their way to the courtyard of the castle. Here, the summer before, they had found the entrance to the well-shaft that ran deep down through the rock, past the dungeons below, beneath the level of the sea, to fresh water.

They all looked about for the well, and came to the old wooden cover. They drew it back.

'There are the rungs of the iron ladder I went down last year,' said Dick, peering in. 'Now, let's find the entrance to the dungeons. The steps down to it are near here.'

They found the entrance, but to their surprise some enormous stones had been pulled across it!

Go to **138.**

147

If you've arrived from **135**, *score* ◁ ◁ ◁.
If you've arrived from **137**, *score* ◁ ◁ ◁ ◁.

'I think we should get the work done now,' said Julian. 'Let's go and have a look at the castle first, and decide where we want to put everything.'

They went right to the very end of the inlet, climbed up on to the rocks and made their way towards the old ruined castle, whose walls rose up from the middle of the island. They stopped to gaze at it.

'It's a fine old ruin,' said Dick. 'Aren't we lucky to have an island and a castle of our own! Fancy, this is all ours!'

They gazed through a broken-down archway to old steps beyond. The castle had once had two fine towers, but now one was almost gone. The other rose high in the air, half-ruined. The jackdaws collected there.

The courtyard was full of big rabbits, which eyed them as they came near. Timmy would have loved to chase them, but George had her hand on his collar and gave him a stern glance.

The children made their way to the little room that they had used the previous summer. It was the only place in the castle that had a sound roof, and they were planning to sleep there.

'Here it is!' said Julian. Then he groaned. 'Oh, blow!' he said. 'We can't use this! The roof's fallen in since last summer. We'll have to find somewhere else to sleep.'

Go to **141.**

Timmy slid down out of the prow of the boat and landed with a surprised *'Woof!'* at Dick's feet. The boat was still swinging wildly as George tried to take the oars from Julian.

'For goodness' sake, Julian,' shouted George, 'stop being so jolly stubborn and give me the oars!'

'No!' yelled Julian.

Anne was getting rather frightened as the boat lurched backwards and forwards on the water.

'Oh, please stop,' she begged the others. 'The boat will capsize and all our supplies will fall in the water and we won't be able to go to Kirrin Island after all. Please stop!' She started to cry.

But Julian and George were so busy struggling, and so cross with each other, that they didn't listen to Anne.

Suddenly the boat gave an extra large lurch, and with a huge splash George fell into the water!

Go to **144.**

He lay on the rocks, still clutching the rope and feeling as though all the breath had been knocked out of him.

'Dick! Are you all right?' asked Anne. 'Have you hurt yourself?'

Dick sat up slowly. He hadn't fallen very far, but

the rocks were sharp. 'My legs hurt,' he said, 'but the rest of me seems to be all right.'

'Stand up,' said George. 'See if you can walk.'

Dick stood up and took a couple of steps.

'No, no bones broken,' he said with a weak grin.

'Well, I think we'd better find a stronger post to attach the rope to,' said Julian. 'That one was obviously rotten.'

They walked along the side of the ship until they came to the bow, where a thick, strong-looking post stuck out.

'Let's try this,' said Julian.

Go to **163.**

150

'What is it?' asked Julian, turning to look out to sea. Then he got a shock! Sticking up out of the water was something that looked rather like a person's head, with fronds of seaweed hanging down around it. Julian stared at it. It seemed to be a human head – and yet the features were blurred and strange-looking.

'Perhaps it's the ghost of a drowned person,' said Anne with a shiver.

Just then the head began to rise even further out of the water, to be followed by George's head and shoulders! She was waving the head in the air and grinning at them.

'I bet that scared you all!' she shouted.

Go to **137.**

If you've arrived from **140**, *score* ⌒⊲ ⌒⊲.

The two girls and Dick went back to where Julian was standing in the courtyard.

'Look!' said Julian, pointing to something on the ground. 'Look! Someone *has* been here! This is where they built a fire!'

Everyone gazed at the ground. There was a heap of wood-ash there, quite obviously left from a fire. There was absolutely no doubt about it – someone had been on the island!

'Whoever it was, they'd better not try coming back,' said George. 'If they do, I'll set Timmy on them!' At the mention of his name, Timmy pricked up his ears and looked all around, but there was no one for him to chase.

'Let's go and see if we can get to the wreck,' said Julian. 'The tide should be off the rocks by now.'

They made their way over the castle wall and down the line of rocks that ran out seawards towards the wreck.

'Here we are,' said Julian at last, and he put his hand on the side of the old wreck.

'How can we get up on to her?' asked George.

'I've got a rope,' said Julian, untying a rope that had been wound around his waist. 'I'll make a loop and see if I can throw it over that post sticking out up there.'

'Bet you can't manage it,' said George.

If you think George is right, go to **163**.
If you think she isn't, go to **157**.

'Yes, that's important,' agreed Julian. 'I'll take first watch. The best place would be up on the cliff above this cave.'

Dick and George went to get the heather, and Julian climbed up the knotted rope. He pulled himself out on to the cliff and sat there. He could see nothing out to sea at all except for some big ocean liner on the horizon. He lay down in the sun, enjoying the warmth. This lookout job was going to be very nice!

He could hear Anne singing down in the cave as she tidied up. She was obviously enjoying herself. He propped himself up on his elbow and scanned the sea lazily. Then he sat up.

'There's something out there,' he said to himself. 'And it looks as though it might be coming this way!'

If you think the ship is coming towards the island, go to **159**.
If you think it sails straight on, go to **166**.

'I'm going back to the cave,' said George. 'I think you must have made a mistake. Come on!'

Julian got to his feet and walked over towards the hole, but just as he picked up the rope he looked back towards the wreck.

Go to **161**.

They hurried up as fast as they could, slipping and sliding on the sloping deck. Anne was standing where they had left her, her eyes shining brightly. She was pointing to something on the opposite side of the ship.

'What is it?' asked George. 'What's the matter?'

'Look – that wasn't here when we came before, surely?' said Anne.

The others looked towards where she pointed. On the deck was an open locker. Inside was a tarpaulin, and sticking out from underneath it was the corner of something that looked as if it were made of metal.

'It looks as though it's a tin trunk of some sort,' said George.

'I think it looks more like a petrol can,' said Julian.

If you think it's a tin trunk, go to **160.**
If you think it's a petrol can, go to **168.**

'What's up?' asked George, pushing behind him. 'Do get on!'

'Isn't that a cave, just beyond that big rock there?' said Dick, pointing. 'If it is, it would be a lovely place to store our things in, and even to sleep in if it were out of reach of the sea.'

'There aren't any caves on this side of Kirrin,'

said George, and then she stopped short. What Dick was pointing at really did look like a cave. After all, George had never explored this line of rocks, and so hadn't been able to catch sight of the cave that lay just beyond. It couldn't possibly be seen from the land.

'Let's go and see,' she said. So they changed direction and cut across the mass of rock towards the cave. As they came near, the cave was hidden behind a jutting-out part of the cliff.

'I think it's just beyond this big rock,' said Dick.

'No, I'm sure it's further on,' said George.

If you think Dick is right, go to **162.**
If you think George is right, go to **167.**

156

They all fell asleep quickly and dreamed of many things. Then suddenly Julian awoke with a jump. Some strange noise had awakened him. He lay still, listening.

Timmy was growling deeply, right down in his throat. '*G-r-r-r-r,*' he went. '*G-r-r-r-r-r!*'

George awoke too, and put out her hand. 'What's the matter, Timmy?' she said.

'He's heard something,' said Julian in a low voice. 'I'm going out to see if I can see anything.'

He scrambled up the rope and climbed on to the cliff. It was a very dark night, and he couldn't even see the wreck. Then suddenly he thought he caught sight of something. It was a light, a good way beyond the line of rocks – just about where the wreck was!

'George! Come up!' he called softly. 'I can see a light on the wreck!'

George shinned up the rope like a monkey and sat down on the cliff beside Julian. They both stared hard towards the wreck, but there was now no sign of a light.

'You must have been mistaken,' said George at last. 'It was a passing ship, perhaps. Let's go back down.'

'I'm *sure* I saw a light,' said Julian. 'I think we should wait a bit longer.' He stared towards the wreck.

If you think they should stay where they are, go to **161**.
If you think they should go back to the cave, go to **153**.

157

Julian threw the rope up once, and missed. But the second time he tried, the rope fell neatly around the post.

'Well done,' said George.

'Now, who's going to climb up first?' said Julian. 'I think I ought to stay here so that I can help Anne up, so either you or George ought to go first, Dick.'

'Let me go first!' said Dick eagerly. 'Do you mind, George?'

George shook her head, so Dick took hold of the rope and started to pull himself up. He hadn't gone more than half way when there was a loud crack, and the post around which the rope was looped broke. Dick fell backwards on to the rocks!

Go to **149**.

158

The sun was pouring into the cave entrance when they woke up next morning.

'I feel sticky and dirty,' said Julian. 'Let's go and have a swim before breakfast.'

They all put on their swimming-costumes and ran out to the little patch of beach outside the cave.

'Look! There's a simply marvellous pool in the middle of those rocks over there!' called Julian. 'It's like a small swimming-pool.'

It really was a lovely rock pool, clear and deep. They splashed about in it, swimming and floating, then went back to the cave with huge appetites for breakfast.

After breakfast Anne said she would arrange all their things neatly in the cave.

'While Anne's doing that,' said George, 'we can go and get some heather for beds – the sand gets a bit hard after a while. And what about keeping a watch on the old wreck, to see who comes there?'

Go to **152**.

He stared hard at the vessel. It was travelling rather fast, and as it came nearer Julian could see that it was a very powerful motor-launch.

I wish I had a pair of binoculars, he thought. Then I'd be able to see who's at the wheel.

But no matter how he strained his eyes, he couldn't make out the face of the helmsman. The motor-launch was quite close to the island, and Julian began to think that whoever was in the boat was going to land in the inlet, but suddenly the boat swerved sharply and headed off out to sea.

'That's odd,' Julian said to himself. 'I wonder if whoever was in that boat *was* intending to land on the island, but saw me up here and decided not to. A fast boat like that would be just what a smuggler would need. Hello – what's this?'

Another boat came chugging into view from around the side of the island.

Go to **166.**

160

George pulled the metal object out. 'I was right!' she declared. It was a small tin trunk bound with leather straps.

'This certainly wasn't here last time we were on the wreck,' said Julian. 'It's not been here very long, either – it's quite dry and new. Whoever does it belong to? And why should it be here?'

They were all amazed at their discovery. Why should anyone put a trunk on the wreck?

'Smugglers, do you think?' asked Dick, his eyes gleaming.

'Yes, it might be,' replied Julian thoughtfully, trying to undo the straps of the trunk. 'This would be a very good place for smugglers. Ships that knew the way could anchor off the island, cast off a boat with smuggled goods, leave them here and go on their way, knowing that people could come and collect the goods at their leisure.'

'Do you think there are smuggled goods inside the trunk?' asked Anne in excitement. 'What might there be? Diamonds?'

'It could be anything that has to have duty paid on it before it can come into the country,' said Julian. 'Blow these straps! I can't undo them!'

Go to **165.**

161

If you've arrived from **153**, *score* ◯⫞.

'Look!' hissed Julian. 'There it is again!'

'Yes – that's someone on our wreck, with a lantern!' said George excitedly. 'I wonder if it's the smugglers, coming to bring more things.'

'Or somebody fetching that trunk,' said Julian. 'Well, we'll know tomorrow, as we'll go and see. Look! Whoever is there is moving off now – the light of the lantern is going lower. They must be getting into a boat by the side of the wreck. Now the light's gone out.'

They strained their ears to hear if they could discover the splash of oars or the sound of voices over the water. They both thought they could hear voices.

'The boat must have gone off to join a ship,' said Julian. 'I believe I can see a faint light right out at sea. Maybe the boat is going to it.'

There was nothing more to see or hear, and soon the two of them slid down the knotted rope back to the cave.

Go to **169.**

162

If you've arrived from **167**, *score* ◯ꞈ.

As they came around the cliff, they saw the cave ahead of them. Steep rocks guarded the entrance and half hid it. Except from where Dick had seen it, it really was impossible to catch sight of it, it was so well hidden.

'It *is* a cave,' said Dick in delight, stepping into it. 'And quite a big one, at that.'

It really was a beauty. Its floor was spread with fine white sand, as soft as powder and perfectly dry, for the cave was clearly higher than the tide reached, except, possibly, in a bad winter storm. Around one side of it ran a stone ledge.

'Exactly like a shelf made just for us!' cried Anne happily. 'We can put all our things here. How lovely! Let's come and live here and sleep here. And look, Julian – we've even got a skylight in the roof!'

She pointed upwards, and the others saw that the roof of the cave was open at one place, giving on to the cliff-top itself. It was plain that somewhere on the heathery cliff above was a hole that looked down to the cave.

'We could drop all our things down through that hole,' said Julian. 'It's not all that high. The cliffs are quite low just here.'

The next thing to do, of course, was to go up on the cliff and find the hole that led to the roof of the cave. They had to search through several clumps of brambles.

'I've found it!' shouted Julian and George at the same time.

If you think George has found it, go to **170.**
If you think Julian has found it, go to **176.**

163

If you've arrived from **149**, *score* ◁ ◁.

Julian threw the rope two or three times, but couldn't get the loop over the post. George took it from him impatiently. At the first throw she got it around the post. She was very good indeed at things like that.

She was up the rope like a monkey, and soon stood on the sloping, slippery deck. Julian helped Anne up, and then the two boys followed.

'It's a horrid smell, isn't it?' said Anne, wrinkling her nose. 'I don't think I'll go and look down in the cabins like we did last time. The smell would be worse there.'

The others left Anne up on the half-rotten deck while they went to explore. But as soon as they got down there, it was obvious that not only could they not sleep there, they couldn't store anything there either. The whole place was damp and rotten.

They were just going up again when they heard a shout from Anne.

'I say! Come here, quickly! I've found something!'

Go to **154.**

164

The sand was very soft, and Timmy didn't hurt himself at all jumping down the hole. He gave himself a shake and barked joyfully.

Then came the business of lowering down all the goods. Anne and Dick tied the things together in rugs, and Julian lowered them carefully. George untied the rope as soon as it reached her, and then back went the rope to be tied around another bundle.

'Last one!' said Julian, after a long spell of really hard work. 'Our next job is to have a really good meal. I'm starving.'

They were very sleepy by the time they had finished supper, so the rugs and cushions were spread out on the floor of the cave, and they were all soon fast asleep.

Go to **158**.

165

If you've arrived from **173**, *score* ◯⊃.

'Let *me* try,' said Anne, who had very deft fingers.

She began to work at the buckles, and in a short time had the straps undone. But a further disappointment awaited them. The trunk was well and truly locked! There were two good locks, and no keys!

'We mustn't smash it open,' said Julian, 'because that would warn whoever it belongs to that the goods had been found. We don't want to let the smugglers know that we've discovered their little game. We want to try to catch them!'

'This is going to be awfully exciting,' said Dick. 'We always seem to have adventures when we come to Kirrin.'

'I think we ought to be getting back over the rocks,' said Julian, suddenly looking over the side of the ship and seeing that the tide had turned. 'Come on – we don't want to be caught by the tide and have to stay here for hours and hours!'

They were soon climbing over the rocks again. Just as they reached the last stretch of rocks leading to the rocky cliff of the island itself, Dick stopped.

Go to **155**.

If you've arrived from **159**, *score* ⌒⌐.

Julian watched the boat – a small trawler – as it chugged along, but after a minute or two it was obvious that the little vessel was going past the island, and he lay down again.

The rest of the day went by pleasantly and lazily. They all took turns at being lookouts, though Anne was severely scolded by Julian for falling asleep during her afternoon watch. No strange vessel appeared, which was disappointing. They badly wanted to know who had put that trunk on the wreck, and why, and what it contained.

'Better go to bed now,' said Julian, when the sun sank low. 'It's about nine o'clock.'

Go to **156**.

They climbed around the big outcrop of rock, but there was no sign of the cave.

'That's funny,' said Dick. 'When we were over on the rocks, the cave looked as if it were just the other side of that bit of cliff that sticks out.'

'No,' said Julian. 'I think it was just the other

side of that *next* piece of rock. We'll have to go a bit further.'

'Oh, please, couldn't we stop for a while to get our breath back?' begged Anne. 'My legs ache dreadfully!'

'Yes, of course,' said Julian. 'But we mustn't stop for too long, because it's getting late.'

After a few minutes they set off to see if the cave was beyond the next part of the cliff.

Go to **162.**

168

George lifted up the tarpaulin, and underneath was a petrol can.

'Why on earth should there be a petrol can on the wreck?' asked Anne in astonishment.

'Somebody might have come out here in a motor-boat, used the petrol from this can to fill its tank, and left the can here,' suggested Dick. 'After all, it's obvious that somebody has been on the island, because of the fire we found in the castle.'

'But *why*?' said George. 'Trippers wouldn't climb on to the wreck, would they? After all, it really isn't very safe.'

'Well, whoever was there left something else as well,' said Julian. 'Look!'

Go to **173.**

Anne and Dick were most indignant the next morning when they heard Julian's tale.

'You *might* have woken us!' said Dick crossly.

'We would have done if there'd been anything much to see,' said George. 'But there was only just the light from a lantern, and nothing else, except that we thought we heard the sound of voices.'

When the tide was low enough the four of them and Timmy set off across the rocks to the wreck. They clambered up and stood on the slanting, slippery deck. They looked towards the locker where the tin trunk had stood. The door of the locker was shut this time. Julian tried to pull it open. Someone had stuffed a piece of wood in to

keep the locker from swinging open. Julian pulled it out, and the door opened easily.

'Anything in there?' asked George.

Go to **174.**

170

'I'm sure this is it,' said George, pulling at the brambles. 'I don't think it's as big as it looked from inside the cave, though. We may not be able to get down through it after all.'

The others looked at her in dismay. If they had to bring all their stuff across the rocks from the boat to the cave, it would take a very long time indeed.

George continued to pull at the brambles. Suddenly she started to laugh. 'What's so funny?' asked Dick.

Go to **176.**

171

'Sh!' said Julian at once. 'Get down behind this bush. Quick, everyone!'

They had left the cove and were walking towards the castle when Timmy growled. Now they all crouched behind a mass of brambles, their hearts beating fast.

Julian peeped through the bush, parting the brambles and scratching his hands. He could just see somebody in the courtyard – one person – two people – maybe three. But, even as he looked, they disappeared.

'I believe they've gone down to the dungeons,' he whispered.

'Let's get back to the cave while they're under ground,' said George. 'I'm so afraid Timmy will give the game away by barking.'

'Or we could try to find out what they're doing,' suggested Dick. 'We might even be able to pull the stones back over the dungeon entrance and trap them!'

If you think they should go back to the cave, go to **175.**
If you think they should investigate the intruders, go to **182.**

172

A dog was sniffing about the bushes not far away – and creeping up behind him, all his hackles up, was Timmy! Timmy was stalking the dog as if he were a cat stalking a rabbit! The other dog suddenly heard him and leapt round, facing Timmy. Timmy flung himself on the dog with a howl.

Julian watched in horror, not knowing what to do. The two dogs made a fearful noise, even though they weren't really hurting each other very much.

This will bring the smugglers up, and they'll see Timmy and know there's someone on the island, thought Julian. Oh, blow you, Timmy!

Go to **178.**

Julian was pointing to another open locker on the other side of the deck. Stuffed into it was a small black trunk, made of tin and bound with leather straps. He pulled it out.

'How extraordinary!' exclaimed George. 'Why should anyone put a trunk on the wreck?'

'Smugglers, do you think?' asked Dick.

'Yes – it might be,' replied Julian, trying to undo the straps.

'Do you think there are smuggled goods inside the trunk?' asked Anne in excitement. 'What might there be? Diamonds?'

'Anything that has to have duty paid on it before it can come into the country,' said Julian. 'Blow these straps! I can't get them undone!'

Go to **165.**

'Yes!' said Julian. 'Look! Tins of food! And cups and plates and things – just as if someone else were going to come and live on the island. Isn't it funny? The trunk is still here, too, locked as before. And here are some candles, and a little lamp, and a bundle of rags. What *are* they here for? Perhaps somebody is planning to come and stay on the island while they wait to take in smuggled goods. Well – we shall be on the lookout for them, day or night!'

They left the wreck, feeling excited. Then George had a sudden thought. 'What about our cove, where we put our boat?' she said. 'They might use that cove, you know, if they come in a boat.'

'Well, if anyone came to our cove, they'd see our boat,' said Dick in alarm. 'We'd better hide it, hadn't we?'

They walked back to the cove and had a look around.

'We could pull the boat round this big rock,' suggested George.

'Or, better still, we could bury it in the sand,' suggested Dick. 'Nobody would ever find it if we did that.'

If you think they should hide it behind the rock, go to **179**.
If you think they should bury it, go to **186**.

175

If you've arrived from **180**, *score* ◁ ◁ ◁.

'Come on, then,' said Julian. 'Don't go across the courtyard – make for the shore and we'll scramble around it until we get to the cave. Then one of us can pop up through the hole and hide behind that big gorse bush there to see who the smugglers are. They must have come in by boat, either from the wreck or by rowing through the rocks off-shore.'

The four of them got to the cave at last and went in. But no sooner had Julian shinned up the rope than Timmy disappeared! He ran out of the cave while their backs were turned.

'Timmy!' called George in a low voice. 'Timmy! Where are you?'

'Perhaps he smelt a rabbit and decided to chase it,' suggested Anne. 'You know how he feels about rabbits!'

'Or he might have smelt something else – like an intruder,' suggested Julian.

If you think it was a rabbit that Timmy smelt, go to **181**.
If you think it was something else, go to **187**.

176

If you've arrived from **170**, *score* ⌒⊃.

'It's all right,' said George. 'This isn't the roof hole after all. It's just a rabbit hole!'

'I'm sure this is the hole over here,' said Julian. They all gathered around him in excitement. 'We'll have to clear these brambles away before we can drop our stuff down,' he said, and they set to work.

Once they had cleared the hole they could look right down into the cave quite easily. Then they went back to the boat and began unloading it. They took everything across to the seaward side of the island, where the cave was. Julian took a strong rope and knotted it thickly at intervals. 'To give our feet a hold as we go down,' he explained.

'Let me go down first, and then you can lower all our things to me,' said George. Down she went, hand over hand, her feet easily finding the thick knots. Timmy, who had been whining anxiously at the edge of the hole, watching George sliding away from him, suddenly jumped into the hole and disappeared down it!

Go to **164.**

177

It didn't take Julian and Anne very long to get back to the cave and find the shovel.

'It was clever of George to put the shovel in,' said Anne as they made their way back to the others. 'She really is resourceful, isn't she?'

They took it in turns to use the shovel, except for Anne, who wasn't really tall enough to use it easily. She had brought an empty tin from the cave, though, and used that to scoop the sand out.

After they had been digging for about half an hour, they sat down to have a rest.

'You know, we've been digging very hard for the last thirty minutes,' said Dick, 'and we've only made a tiny hole. I don't think we're going to be able to bury the boat after all.'

'You're right,' said Julian. 'I think we'll have to follow George's original suggestion and pull it up behind that big rock.'

Go to **179.**

From the walls of the ruined castle came three figures, running pell-mell to see what was happening to their dog – and Julian stared at them in the very greatest amazement, for the three people were none other than Mr Stick, Mrs Stick and Edgar!

'Golly!' said Julian, crawling around the bush to get to the hole quickly. 'They've come after us! They've guessed we've come here, and they've come to look for us to make us go back! Well, they won't find us. But what a pity Timmy's given the game away!'

There came a shrill whistle from down below him. It was George. Timmy always obeyed that whistle, and he let go of the other dog at once, just as the three Sticks arrived on the scene and picked up the whining Tinker.

Edgar tore after Timmy, up to the cliff-top, and Julian quickly dropped down into the cave. Timmy ran to the hole and scrambled through it, landing almost on top of Julian.

'Goodness,' said Julian. 'I hope Edgar didn't see Timmy doing his disappearing trick!'

If you think Edgar did see Timmy disappear, go to **184.**
If not, go to **191.**

If you've arrived from **177**, *score* ◁ ◁ ◁.

With much puffing and panting they hauled the boat around the rock, which almost completely hid it.

'Good!' said George, going down into the cove to see if very much of the boat showed. 'A bit of her does still show. Let's cover it with seaweed.'

They draped the prow of the boat with all the seaweed they could find, and after that, unless anyone went deliberately around the big rock, the boat was really not noticeable at all.

'Good!' said Julian, looking at his watch. 'I say – it's long past teatime. And, you know, while we've been doing all this with the boat, we quite forgot to have someone on the lookout post on the cliff-top. What idiots we are!'

'Well, I don't expect anything has happened since we've been away from the cave,' said Dick.

And then Timmy began to growl again!

Go to **171**.

180

Julian made up his mind and began to walk down the stone steps that led to the castle dungeons. He reached the bottom and paused, straining his ears for the sound of voices. The dungeons were full of echoes, and even a whisper sounded much louder down there. But as he listened he realised something. He hadn't got a torch, and exploring the dungeons without one would be impossible. He would be lost within seconds. And at that moment he heard voices coming back through one of the tunnels.

Julian flew up the steps, across the courtyard, and collapsed breathlessly beside the others.

'Did you see anyone?' asked Dick.

Julian shook his head, too puffed to speak.

'I think we'd better go back to the cave, don't you?' asked George.

Go to **175.**

181

But it was a rabbit. Timmy, normally the most obedient of dogs, couldn't resist the rabbits on the island. He knew that there was one nearby, and it was too much for him. He scrambled over the rocks and along to a place where the cliffs dipped down to the sea, and then ran up on to the cliffs above the cave. There he found not one but two lovely big rabbits, peacefully nibbling the grass. However, just as Timmy was about to launch himself at them, he smelt another, unpleasantly familiar smell.

Go to **187.**

'I think it would be a good idea if just one of us went down to investigate,' said Julian. 'We shouldn't all go, because they might be dangerous – even have guns.'

'Goodness,' breathed Anne. 'How frightening!'

'Well, if anybody is going to go, I think it should be me,' said George. 'I would like to see who's been messing about on *my* island.'

'But if you go, then Timmy will want to go too, and he'll bark if he sees anyone strange, especially if they look threatening,' objected Julian. 'No – I think I'd better go on my own. I won't let them spot me!'

Go to **185.**

Go to **185.**

183

After about an hour the children relaxed, thinking that the Sticks must have given up looking for them. They boiled the kettle to make some tea, and Anne cut some sandwiches.

They ate their tea quietly, not speaking above a whisper.

'You know,' said Julian. 'I've thought of something. It's plain they haven't come here to look for us – they thought we'd gone home. So don't you think it's possible the Sticks might be something to do with the smugglers? Mr Stick is a sailor, isn't he? He'd know all about smuggling.'

'I believe you're right,' said George. 'Well – we'll wait until the Sticks have gone, then we'll go down to the dungeons and see if they've hidden anything there!'

Go to **193.**

184

If you've arrived from **188**, *score*

Edgar, panting and puffing, arrived on the cliff-top just in time to see Timmy apparently disappear into the solid earth. He hunted about for a bit, but it was clear that the dog was no longer on the cliff.

Mr and Mrs Stick came up too.

'Where did that dog go?' shouted Mrs Stick. 'What was he like?'

'Like that nasty Timmy, that's what,' said Edgar. His voice could be clearly heard by everyone down in the cave.

'But it *couldn't* be!' objected Mrs Stick. 'The children have gone away – we saw them, *and* the dog, too, making off towards the railway. It must be some sort of stray dog left here by a tripper.'

Go to **190.**

185

Julian got up from behind the bramble bush and started to walk forwards slowly. The others stayed where they were, George with her hand on Timmy's collar. Julian moved towards the courtyard as quietly and quickly as he could.

When he came closer he could see that whoever was on the island had moved the big stones that had been pulled over the entrance to the dungeons.

'That settles it,' he said to himself. 'It *must* be smugglers. No one else would want to get into the dungeons.'

He moved on into the courtyard and looked at the dungeon entrance. Should he risk going down and having a look?

Go to **180.**

186

'I think we'd better bury it,' said Julian. 'After all, we don't want there to be the slightest chance of anyone finding the boat and knowing that we're on the island. Let's pull it a bit further up first.'

The four of them pulled and pushed at the boat, and had soon moved it quite a lot further up the beach of the little inlet.

'Right!' said Julian. 'Now to cover it with sand.'

They started to scoop sand up the sides of the boat, but all that happened was that it slid off again!

'This is no good,' said Dick. 'We obviously can't bury the boat like this. 'We'll have to dig a hole.'

'But that will take *hours*,' objected George. 'We've only got our hands to dig with.'

'I know what we could use,' said Anne.

Go to **189.**

187

If you've arrived from **181,** *score* ⌓.

George walked to and fro outside the cave, calling, but Timmy wasn't listening. He had smelt something important: a smell he knew – a dog smell – and he meant to find the owner of it!

Julian sat close beside the gorse bush, watching all around. There was nothing to be seen on the wreck, and there was no ship out to sea. Probably the boat that brought the strangers to the castle was hidden down below among the rocks. Julian looked behind him, towards the castle – and even as he looked he saw an astonishing sight!

Go to **172.**

'That dog is in that clump of gorse bushes over there!' he said.

Mr Stick looked at him.

'I'm beginning to think that you're going barmy, my lad!' he said. 'There is no dog on this island apart from Tinker, understand?'

'I saw him,' said Edgar stubbornly. 'I saw a black and white face peering out from the clump of bushes over there.'

Mr Stick sighed heavily.

'It must have been a badger,' he said. 'Haven't you never seen a badger? They have black and white faces. That's what you saw. Now come on.'

Edgar walked along behind his parents, looking sulky. Timmy decided that he had played his game for long enough and began to slink back towards the cave. But unfortunately, just as he got to the clump of brambles that hid the hole down into the cave, Edgar turned around and saw him.

'Hey!' shouted Edgar, and started to run.

Go to **184**.

The others looked at her.

'When I was putting all the stuff away in the cave yesterday I found a small shovel. We could use that!' said Anne.

'Anne! Well done!' said Dick. 'But why on earth

did anyone bother bringing a shovel to the island?'

'I put it in,' said George. 'I thought we might have rubbish – tins and things like that – that we would have to bury. After all, we don't want to leave rubbish on our beautiful island, and if we wait until we go home to deal with it, it'll get very smelly, especially if the weather goes on being so lovely and hot.'

'Well, the shovel sounds like just what we need to dig a hole to bury the boat in,' said Julian. 'I'll go and get it.'

'I'll come with you,' offered Anne. 'I know where it is, and I don't want you turning every-thing upside down looking for it!'

'All right, then,' said Julian. 'Dick and George, you stay here and keep a sharp lookout for any approaching boats.'

Dick and George sat down on the sand to wait, and Julian and Anne set off back to the cave.

Go to **177**.

190

'Well, where is he, then?' said Mr Stick's hoarse voice. 'Can't see no dog anywhere about now.'

'He disappeared into the earth,' answered Edgar in a surprised voice.

Mr Stick made a rude and scornful noise. 'You tell lovely tales, you do,' he said. 'Disappeared into the earth! What next? Fell over the cliff, I should think.'

'If it *is* the children's dog, then those tiresome kids must have come to this island instead of going home,' said Mrs Stick. 'That would upset our plans all right! We shall have to find out.'

'We can easily do that,' said Mr Stick. 'Their boat will be here somewhere – and they'll be about too. 'We'll split up and look for them.'

Edgar was half scared of finding the children, so he didn't make much of a search for either the children or the boat. He went into the cove where the boat had been pulled up, but he didn't notice the seaweedy prow of the boat sticking out from the rock behind which it was hidden.

'Nothing here!' he called to his mother, who was looking around the ruins. Mr Stick found nothing, either.

'Couldn't have been the children's dog,' said Mr Stick at last. 'They'd be here, if it were, and so would their boat. That dog must have been a stray.'

Go to **183**.

191

Timmy crouched down on the floor of the cave next to George.

'Keep quiet,' said George to the excited dog. 'Do you want to give our hiding-place away?'

Timmy wagged his tail, then sat quietly beside George. Nearby, they could hear the Sticks' voices, but not what they were saying.

Suddenly Tinker started to bark, and it was too much for Timmy. Before George could stop him, he was out of the cave and running along the rocks back to the path that led to the cliff-top. George couldn't shout for him or whistle in case the Sticks might hear and find their hiding-place.

Timmy bounded on to the cliff-top and stood for a moment, his head cocked to one side, watching the Sticks, who were standing in a huddle, talking urgently.

Just then Edgar turned around.

Go to **194.**

192

'Whoo-whoo-whoo!' called Julian again.

The flicker of light from Mr Stick's candle seemed to stop, then grow fainter. Finally it disappeared. Julian grinned to himself in the dark. Mr Stick had obviously decided to go back to the safety of the dungeon with the wooden door. Then Julian had an idea. He would give Mr Stick one more jolly good fright!

Moving as quickly as he could, silent in his rubber-soled shoes, he ran back along the side tunnel until he came to the main passage. He could just see the glimmer of Mr Stick's candle as he scurried back to Edgar and Mrs Stick.

Julian crept up behind him, as close as he dared, and then shouted at the top of his voice: *'Boo!'*

The word echoed all around, sounding enormously loud. Mr Stick gave a yell of terror and rushed madly up the passage towards the dungeon with the wooden door.

'That should make sure they don't come out until morning!' he said to himself, and went back to the dungeon entrance to join the others.

Go to **196.**

193

But the Sticks didn't go! The children peeped out of the spy-hole at the top of the cave roof every now and again, and saw one or other of the Sticks. Julian ran down to the nearby shore and discovered a small boat there. So the Sticks had managed to find their way around the rocks.

'It looks as if they've come to stay the night,' said Julian gloomily. 'This is going to spoil our stay here, all right.'

'Let's frighten them,' suggested George, her eyes shining.

'What do you mean?' asked Dick, cheering up. 'What's your idea?'

'Couldn't we creep down and do a bit of shouting, so that the echoes start up all around?' said George. 'You know how frightening we found the echoes when we first went down to the dungeons.'

'*What* a good idea!' said Julian. 'Come on, let's go now.'

There was no sign of the Sticks at the ruined castle, but the stones weren't over the dungeon entrance. The children felt sure the Sticks were down there.

'What noises could we make?' asked Dick. 'Let's be animals! I can moo jolly well.'

'I think we should be smugglers – or pirates. We could shout "Yo ho ho and a bottle of rum!"' said George.

If you think they should make animal noises, go to **198**.
If you think they should be pirates, go to **203**.

194

He gave a shout of surprise. 'Look! There's that dog again!'

But Timmy was too quick. He darted behind a large clump of gorse bushes. The Sticks looked at Edgar.

'You've got dogs on the brain, you have,' said Mr Stick. 'I can't see no dog. You're just imagining things.'

'I saw him,' said Edgar stubbornly. 'And it was that dog of the children's. I'd know that dog anywhere.'

Timmy crouched silently behind the bush, waving his tail gently. He was going to have some fun with the Sticks now!

'Let's go back to the castle,' said Mr Stick. 'There's a fair bit we need to do in those dungeons before tonight.'

From behind his bush Timmy gave a tiny
'*Woof!*'

Go to **197.**

195

However, just as they were about to shout at the
tops of their voices, George caught Dick's eye and
started to giggle. They all looked so funny with
their mouths wide open!

'Ss-sh, George!' said Julian. 'This isn't funny.'

But George, now that she had started to laugh,
couldn't stop. The sight of George helpless with
laughter was so infectious that first Anne, then
Dick, then finally Julian began to laugh too.

'Come on,' said Julian, as soon as he could
speak, 'I think we'd better go back to the cave and
calm down, and then decide what we should do.'

They made their way back to the cave.

'Should we still try to be pirates?' asked Anne. 'I
bet we'll start to laugh again if we do.'

Go to **198.**

196

If you've arrived from **192,** *score* ◁ ◁ ◁.
If you've arrived from **205,** *score* ◁ ◁ ◁ ◁ ◁.

Mr Stick went quickly back into the dungeon and
shut the big wooden door. His hands were shaking.

'Very odd goings on,' he said. 'Shan't stay here

much longer if we get this sort of thing happening every night.'

Julian, Dick and George stumbled up the dungeon steps, helpless with giggles. They told Anne everything that had happened, which made Anne laugh, too. Then they made their way back to the cave.

When they got back to the hole in the cliff-top, Julian stood by it, shining his torch so that the others could see to climb down the rope. Before going down it himself he glanced up, looking out over the dark sea, and then stared intently.

There was a light out to sea, and it was signalling. It must have seen his torchlight! It went on for a long time, as if a message were being flashed. Julian wondered whether to send a message back. He had learned Morse Code in the Scouts. Or should he just ignore it, go down into the cave and go to sleep?

If you think he should answer the signal, go to **202.**
If you think he should ignore it, go to **208.**

197

Mrs Stick looked around. Timmy kept quiet.

'What do you think we should do about supper, Ma?' asked Edgar. 'I'm really . . . what was that?'

Timmy gave another tiny *'Woof!'*

'I heard a dog barking,' said Edgar.

'You really have got a thing about dogs today,'

said Mr Stick. 'If you heard a dog barking, it was probably Tinker. Now come on back to the castle.'

The Sticks set off back across the cliff. Timmy waited a moment, then, keeping very low, he ran along the cliff, parallel to where the Sticks were walking but out of their sight behind a small fold in the ground. He ran on swiftly until he was in front of them, then hid behind another gorse bush. As the Sticks drew level with his hiding-place, he stuck his head around the side and looked at them.

Edgar stopped dead.

Go to **188**.

198

If you've arrived from **206**, *score* �◁ ◁.
If you've arrived from **195**, *score* ◁ ◁ ◁ ◁.

'I think we should be animals,' said Julian. 'I'm sure that would be more convincing.'

'Perhaps I'll stay here with Timmy,' said Anne suddenly. She didn't like the dark dungeons at all.

The others chuckled. They knew Anne was frightened. Julian squeezed her arm.

'You do that, then,' he said. 'You keep old Timmy company. Now – have we all got our torches? We must be careful to use them only when we absolutely must. We don't want the Sticks to see us.'

Julian, Dick and George made their way down the long flight of steps that led to the deep old dungeons of Kirrin Castle. When they reached the bottom they set off down one of the winding passages that led in and out of the dungeons cut out of the rock below the castle. Before they had gone very far, George suddenly put up a warning hand. They all stood very still.

Go to **201.**

199

Julian ran a short way down the tunnel, and then paused for breath. Looking back down the tunnel he could just see a flicker of light, which meant that Mr Stick was coming. Julian took a deep breath. *'Whoo-whoo-whoo!'* he went.

The dungeons picked up the noise and echoed it around the passages, making it sound as if a whole army of ghosts were in the tunnel.

Julian chuckled quietly and made his noise again.

Go to **192.**

200

'First of all I'll moo again, to make Mr Stick come down here, then we'll both whistle – like the wind does. You know – *whee-whee-whee!*' said Dick.

'Suppose he hears you mooing and decides not to come down here after all?' asked George.

'Then we shall have to get rid of him anyway,' said Dick cheerfully. 'I'm going to have a look down the passage to see if I can see anything.'

He walked to the end of the passage and looked cautiously around into the main corridor.

'He's coming,' he hissed to George. 'I'm going to moo.'

George giggled as Dick made a mooing noise that sounded exactly as if a herd of cows were wandering about in the dungeons. Dick, peering around the end of the passage, saw the light of Mr Stick's candle coming nearer and nearer.

'Right,' he said. 'I'm going into the passage opposite. I'll whistle first, then you.'

Go to **205**.

201

There was a light ahead in one of the dungeons, and they could hear voices.

'They're in that room where we found the treasure last year!' whispered George. 'What noises shall we make?'

'I'll be a cow,' said Dick. 'I can moo awfully like a cow.'

'I'll be a sheep,' said Julian. 'George, you could be a horse. You can whinny just like a horse. Go on, Dick. You begin.'

Hidden behind a rocky pillar, Dick opened his mouth and mooed dolefully, like a cow in pain. At once the echoes took up the mooing, magnified it, sent it along all the underground passages, until it seemed as if a thousand cows had wandered in there and were mooing together.

'*Moo-oo-oo-OOOO, ooo-oo-MOOOOOOOO!*'

The Sticks listened in astonishment and fright at the awful noise.

'What is it, Ma?' said Edgar, almost in tears. Tinker crouched at the back of the cave, terrified.

Go to **209.**

202

Julian watched the signalling carefully for a little while longer. He thought he could make out the word 'wreck', which in Morse Code went 'dot dash dash/dot dash dot/dot/dash dot dash dot/dash dot dash', and also the words 'Next day', but the rest of it wasn't clear.

He decided to signal back 'All well', because if whoever was sending the signal had seen his torch, and didn't get a reply, he might think something was wrong. So Julian very carefully flashed dot dash/dot dash dot dot/dot dash dot dot/dot dash dash/dot/dot dash dot dot/dot dash dot dot', and then added 'dot dot dot/dash/dot dot/dash dot dash dot/dash dot dash', which in Morse Code meant 'Stick'.

There was another series of flashes from the ship. This time Julian was able to start reading the message right from the beginning.

Go to **212.**

203

'Let's be pirates, then,' said Julian. 'That would really frighten the Sticks. I know – we can shout "Sixteen men on a dead man's chest!" That's another pirate saying.'

'I think it would be a good idea if we practised first,' said Dick. 'Then we can make it sound really frightening.'

'Well, we can't practise here,' said Julian. 'The Sticks might hear us. We'd better go back to the cave and do it there.'

'Right!' said Julian, when they were in the cave, safely out of earshot. 'All together now!'

The children all shouted at the tops of their voices:

'*Sixteen men on a dead man's chest! Yo ho ho and a bottle of rum!*'

Timmy barked loudly, which was his way of joining in.

Go to **206.**

204

Mr Stick went back quickly into the dungeon and lit another candle. Then he walked out into the passage.

'Who's there? Come out! Stop this noise!' he shouted.

'*Noise-oise-oise-oise,*' went the echoes. The children were all stifling their giggles.

George shouted out in a very deep, gruff voice: '*Beware!*' and the echoes thundered out all around. '*'Ware! 'Ware! 'Ware-are-are!*'

Mr Stick began to walk down the passage, the candle held high.

'Quick!' Julian whispered to George. 'Let's split up, so that he won't know who to chase. You go with Dick, and I'll go on my own.'

George and Dick set off back down the passage, and Julian dodged into one of the small tunnels that lay to one side.

Mr Stick thought he heard footsteps, and wondered whether to go straight on or explore the side tunnel.

If you think he goes straight on, go to **213.**
If you think he explores the side tunnel, go to **199.**

Mr Stick walked up the passage feeling rather shaken. He was sure there were no cows on the island, and yet he had heard them in the dungeons! He could see very little in the dark passage, as the candle didn't give much light, and he didn't notice the two side passages in which Dick and George were hiding. Suddenly he heard the most extraordinary shrieking sound, as if all the devils in hell were in the dungeons with him.

'Wheeeeeee-wheeeee-wheeeeeee!' it went. 'Whee-wheeeeee!'

Mr Stick turned and ran back to the dungeon with the wooden door, where Mrs Stick and Edgar were waiting.

Dick and George waited for a minute or two, then made their way back to the dungeon entrance to meet Julian.

Go to **196.**

206

'Let's try it once more,' said Julian.

They all shouted again, as loudly as they could: 'Sixteen men on a dead man's chest! Yo ho ho and a bottle of rum!'

Julian looked a bit thoughtful. 'You know, I think we don't really sound very convincing. Our voices are too high. Real pirates have much deeper voices. We'd better try again and see if we can make our voices deeper.'

They all shouted again, trying to make their voices as deep as possible. Julian could manage it quite easily, but Dick and George could only lower their voices a little bit, and Anne not at all.

Julian still wasn't very happy. 'I wonder whether we ought to be animals after all,' he said, as they walked back towards the castle. 'Otherwise I think the Sticks might be suspicious and guess that it's us, and we certainly don't want that!'

'Oh, I'm sure they'll be so frightened that they'll never think that it might be us,' said Dick. 'Let's try it!'

If you think they should be animals after all, go to **198.**
If you still think they should be pirates, go to **210.**

207

'We'd better not stand here in the passage and discuss it,' said Dick. 'If I remember, if we walk on a bit down here, there are a couple of side passages. We'd better hide in one of those.'

Further on they came to the passage that Dick had remembered.

'Now, what shall we do to frighten Mr Stick?' asked George.

Dick thought for a moment. 'I know,' he said. 'We'll make a noise, something to lure him down to this part of the dungeons. Then if I stand at the end of this passage we're in, but just out of sight, and if you go across to that passage opposite, and we both say the same thing, one after the other, then the echoes will make the noise seem to be coming from all around Mr Stick. That should confuse him nicely!'

'That's a *super* idea,' said George. 'Now, what shall we say?'

Go to **200.**

208

'Perhaps they're going to put more stuff into the old wreck for the Sticks to find,' Julian said to himself. 'I wonder if they are. I'd like to find out – but it would be dangerous to go there in daylight in case the Sticks see us.'

Obviously the signalling was a message of some sort for the Sticks, but Julian didn't think they would leave the dungeon until daylight – they'd be too scared of all the strange animals that were rushing about in the dungeons!

He dropped down the rope into the cave.

Go to **217.**

209

'It's cows,' said Mr Stick, amazed. 'Them there's cows. How did cows get to be here?'

'Nonsense!' said Mrs Stick, recovering herself a little. 'Cows down in these caves! You're mad. You'll be telling me there's sheep next!'

It was funny that she should have said that, for

Julian chose that moment to begin baa-ing like a flock of sheep.

Mr Stick jumped to his feet, white as a sheet.

'Well, if it isn't sheep now!' he said. 'What's up? What's in these 'ere dungeons? I never did like 'em.'

'*Baa-aa-AAAAAAAAAA!*' went the mournful bleats all round and about.

Poor Tinker began to whine pitifully.

Mr Stick went to the door of the room they were in and shouted loudly. 'Get out, you! Clear out, whoever you are!'

George giggled. Mr Stick heard her, and hesitated. Should he stay where he was, safely in the dungeon, or should he go and see who was out there?

If you think Mr Stick stays in the dungeon, go to **196.**
If you think he decides to go and investigate, go to **204.**

210

Moving as quietly as they could, they made their way back into the courtyard of the castle. Anne didn't like the idea of going into the dungeons very much, but she didn't say anything.

They crept down the steps that led to the dungeons and stopped at the bottom.

'Let's start here, then tramp slowly down one of the passages,' suggested Julian. 'That'll sound really spooky.' They moved a few steps away from the bottom of the stairs.

'All right, then,' said Julian. 'One, two, three!'

They all took a deep breath and opened their mouths.

Go to **195.**

211

George and Dick went cautiously and quietly over the cliff to the castle. Edgar appeared out of the ruined room, carrying a pile of cushions that had evidently been stored there. George went red with rage.

'Mother's best cushions!' she whispered. 'Oh, the beasts!'

Dick felt angry too. He picked up a clod of earth and flung it into the air. It fell between Edgar and Tinker, breaking into a shower of earth.

Edgar dropped the cushions and looked up into the air in fright. George threw another clod up high. It fell all over Tinker, who scuttled down into the entrance to the dungeons.

Then Dick gave one of his realistic moos, exactly like a cow in pain, and Edgar stood rooted to the spot, almost frightened out of his skin. Those cows again! Dick mooed once more and Edgar gave a yell, almost falling down the dungeon steps.

Go to **214.**

Knowing Morse Code is jolly useful, Julian thought as he watched the flashing light. He had learnt a lot about Morse in the Scouts, and knew that the dashes were three times the length of the dots, and that a gap equal to two dots was left between each letter.

The message coming back from the ship said only, 'That's all', and then stopped. He waited for a few minutes in case the flashing started again, but eventually he decided that there would be no more signals that night, and dropped down the rope into the cave where the others were waiting.

Go to **217.**

Mr Stick decided he would go straight on down the main passage, towards the dungeon entrance. If there was anybody – or anything – in the dungeons, that would surely be the place they would head for.

Dick and George ran down the tunnel and past the entrance.

'I hope Anne's all right up there on her own,' said Dick.

'She's got Timmy,' said George. 'He'll look after her.

'Stop a mintute, George,' said Dick. 'We ought

to decide what we're going to do. Shall we try to give Mr Stick another good fright?'

'Oh yes, let's,' said George. 'What could we do?'

Go to **207**.

214

'Quick!' said Dick, jumping to his feet. 'He won't be back for a few minutes – he'll be too scared. Let's grab the cushions and bring them here.'

They raced to the courtyard, picked up the cushions and raced back to their hiding-place.

'What about slipping across and seeing what else they've stored in the little room?' suggested Dick.

'Good idea,' said George. 'I'll go, and you stay here and moo if you see Edgar again. That should frighten him back into the dungeons!'

Dick walked quickly to the flight of steps that led under ground. There was no sign of Edgar or Tinker. George went into the little room and gazed around in anger. There were blankets and silver-ware and all kinds of food.

She ran over to Dick.

'There are *heaps* of our things,' she whispered fiercely. 'Come and help me get them before Edgar appears or the Sticks come back.'

Just as they were whispering together, they heard a low whistle. They looked around and saw Julian coming towards them.

Go to **220**.

215

*If you've arrived from **228**, score* ⌒⌒.

Finally Edgar emerged from the dungeons, looking extremely scared.

'Come on!' said Mrs Stick. 'You'd better stay up in the sunshine now.'

'I'm scared,' said Edgar. 'I'm not staying up here alone.'

'Why not?' asked Mr Stick, astonished.

'It's them cows again!' said Edgar. 'Hundreds of them, Pa, all a-mooing around me and throwing things at me. They're dangerous animals, they are, and I'm not coming up here alone!'

The Sticks stared at Edgar as if he were mad.

'Cows throwing things?' said Mrs Stick at last. 'What do you mean by that? Cows can't throw anything.'

'These ones did,' said Edgar. 'Proper scared I was, and so was Tinker. I dropped the cushions I was taking down and rushed away to hide.'

'Where *are* the cushions?' asked Mr Stick, looking around. 'I can't see no cushions.'

'Didn't you take everything down to the dungeons?' demanded Mrs Stick. 'Because that room's empty now. There's not a thing in it.'

'I didn't take nothing down at all,' said Edgar. 'I dropped the cushions just about where you're standing. What's happened to them?'

'I don't know,' said Mr Stick. 'But I'll tell you

what – there's something funny about this. Looks as if there's somebody else on this island!'

Go to **221**.

216

Julian ran to the wall of the castle and climbed on to its crumbling edge. He could see the little inlet and the Sticks moving about on the beach. They were both staring at the ground, as if they were looking for something.

'Hey, can you see it?' he heard Mr Stick shout to Mrs Stick.

'No,' she called back. 'But it must be here somehwere. I put it in my pocket before I got into the boat, and it wasn't there when we got to the wreck. It isn't in the boat, so it *must* be somewhere on the beach.'

Julian was puzzled. What on earth where they looking for? It was obviously important, because they had both got down on their hands and knees to search on the sand.

Go to **223**.

217

If you've arrived from **212**, *score* ◠.

The children slept well that night. In the morning they had a big breakfast, then Dick suggested going to the castle to have a look around.

'We'll have to be careful the Sticks don't see us,' said George.

Anne decided to stay behind and tidy up the cave, so the other three set off, leaving Timmy with Anne in case he barked or whined and gave them away.

They lay flat on the cliff-top, overlooking the castle. As they watched, the Sticks appeared from the dungeons. They spoke together for a moment or two, and then Mr and Mrs Stick went off in the direction of the shore that faced the wreck. Edgar went to the room in which the children had first planned to sleep – the one whose roof had fallen in.

'I'm going to follow the Sticks,' whispered Julian to the others. 'You two see what Edgar is up to.'

If you want to go with George and Dick, go to **211.**
If you want to go with Julian, go to **222.**

218

If you've arrived from **230,** *score* ▱ ▱ ▱.

'We'd better take the trunk back to the cave,' said Julian. 'Come on, Dick, we must hurry!'

Each took a handle of the small trunk and lifted it between them. They staggered back to George with it.

'We'll take it to the cave,' said Julian. 'You stay here a few minutes and see what happens.'

The boys went across the cliff-top with the

trunk. George flattened herself behind a bush and waited. Mr Stick appeared again in a few minutes and looked around for the trunk. His mouth fell open in astonishment when he saw that it was gone. He yelled down the entrance to the dungeon. 'Clara! The trunk's gone!'

Mrs Stick and Edgar appeared from the dungeons and stared at him.

'Gone?' said Mrs Stick in enormous surprise. 'Where's it gone?'

Go to **226.**

Julian was right. The Sticks were on their way back to the castle, carrying the trunk from the wreck.

'Let's follow them, and see what happens when they find everything gone,' said Julian, grinning. 'Come on, everyone!' He called down to Anne: 'We'll be back in a little while.'

They wriggled over the cliff on their stomachs and came to a clump of bushes behind which they could hide and watch. The Sticks put the trunk down and looked around for Edgar. But Edgar was nowhere to be seen.

'Where's that boy?' said Mrs Stick impatiently. 'He's had plenty of time to do everything. Edgar! Edgar! Edgar!'

Mr Stick went to the ruined room and peeped inside.

'He's taken everything down,' he said. 'He must be down in the dungeons.'

'I told him to come up and sit in the sun when he'd finished,' said Mrs Stick. ''Tisn't healthy down in them dungeons. *Edgar!*'

If you think Edgar comes up, go to **215**.
If you think he stays in the dungeons, go to **224**.

If you've arrived from **225**, *score* ⌁ ⌁.

Julian joined Dick and George by the dungeon steps.

'The Sticks have rowed off to the wreck,' he said. 'They've got an old boat somewhere down among those rocks.'

'Oh, then we've got time to do what we want to do,' said Dick, pleased. He told Julian that he and George had been to the ruined room in the castle and found cushions, blankets, silverware and food – all stolen from Kirrin Cottage.

'Awful thieves!' said Julian. 'They don't mean to go back to Kirrin Cottage, that's plain. Well, we'd better hurry if we're going to take the things away. Dick, you keep watch while George and I move everything.'

Go to **227.**

Just then a dismal howl came echoing up from below the ground. It was Tinker, terrified at being alone, and not daring to come up.

'Poor lamb!' said Mrs Stick.

Tinker let out an even more doleful howl, and Mrs Stick hurried down the steps to go to him. Mr Stick followed her, and Edgar lost no time in going after them.

'Quick!' said Julian, standing up. 'Come with

me, Dick. We may just have time to get that trunk.'

'Wait a minute,' said Dick. 'We could use the trunk to block the dungeon entrance and trap the Sticks down there while we have a chance to look inside it. What do you think?'

If you think they should take the trunk away, go to **218**.
If you think they should try to block the dungeon entrance with it, go to **232**.

222

Julian moved along the cliff-top, keeping as low as he could. The Sticks walked down to the place where the rocks began and pulled an old, battered-looking rowing-boat off the rocks and into the water. They both got in, and Mr Stick began to row.

Julian watched until they had reached the wreck. Mr Stick threw a rope over a thick-looking post that jutted out at the bow of the boat, and pulled himself up on to the deck. Then Mrs Stick threw the rope from the rowing-boat up to him, and he tied it up. Mrs Stick scrambled clumsily up the rope on to the wreck.

Well, that's that for a while, thought Julian. I'd better get back to the others.

He got up and began to walk along the cliff-top.

Go to **229**.

The Sticks crawled about the beach, lifting up stones, looking under lumps of seaweed and generally searching the little inlet.

Then suddenly Mr Stick gave a shout of triumph.

'Here it is!' he yelled to Mrs Stick, who was down at the other end of the beach. Mr Stick held up his hand, and Julian could see sunlight glinting on something shiny.

'That's a relief,' called Mrs Stick. 'We'd better get back to the wreck now. But we'd never have got that trunk open without the key!'

So that was what they'd been looking for! The key to open the mysterious little trunk that the children had found on the wreck.

The Sticks got into the boat and started to row out towards the line of rocks where the wreck was lying. Julian scrambled down off the wall and went to tell the others what he had seen.

Go to **233.**

224

But even though the Sticks shouted for Edgar over and over again, he didn't appear.

'I suppose we'll just have to go down into the dungeons and get him,' said Mr Stick. 'I can't think why he doesn't come up. Perhaps he's got lost in that maze of tunnels.'

'Oh, no!' said Mrs Stick. 'And he's got Tinker down there with him. Supposing Tinker gets lost? We'd never find him again. I'd never forgive myself if anything happened to that poor animal!'

The listening children thought that Mrs Stick sounded a great deal fonder of Tinker than she was of Edgar!

Mr and Mrs Stick disappeared down into the dungeons. They left the trunk sitting in the middle of the courtyard.

Go to **228.**

225

Julian scanned the boat through the binoculars. There seemed to be no one about on deck, and there was nobody at the wheel, either. Then, as Julian watched, a man came up from the cabin below and started to move around on the little deck at the stern of the boat. Suddenly the boy realised what the man was doing. He was going to fish over the side of the boat. Julian grinned to himself. So it was nothing sinister at all – just a man enjoying a couple of hours' fishing!

Julian got up and began to walk back to the castle.

Go to **220.**

'That's what *I'd* like to know!' said Mr Stick. 'We leave it here a few minutes – and then it goes. Walks off by itself, just like the other things!'

'Look here, there's someone on this island,' said Mrs Stick. 'And I'm going to find out who it is. Got your gun, Pa?'

'I have,' said Mr Stick, slapping his belt. 'You get a good stout stick too, and we'll take Tinker. If we don't ferret out whoever's trying to spoil our plans, my name's not Stick!'

Go to **236.**

227

George and Julian ran to the ruined room, piled their arms with the goods there, then ran to hide them on the cliff, ready to take them down to the cave when they had time. It looked as if the Sticks had just taken whatever was easiest to lay their hands on. They had even brought the kitchen clock!

Edgar didn't appear at all, so Dick had nothing to do but sit by the steps of the dungeon and watch the others. It took them quite a long time to get all the stuff out of the little room, but just as they were bringing the last few items out, they heard a voice calling, 'Hey!'

'That must be the Sticks coming back,' said Dick. 'We'd better hurry!'

'I thought it sounded more like Anne,' said George. 'We've been gone so long she's probably wondering what's become of us.'

If you think it's the Sticks, go to **216**.
If you think it's Anne, go to **233**.

228

'We could go down and get the trunk while the Sticks are in the dungeons!' said Dick.

'But they might come back and find us,' objected George. 'The last thing we want is for the Sticks to know that we're on the island.'

'It won't take a minute,' argued Dick. 'With any luck, they've unlocked the trunk and we'll be able to see what's inside.'

'What do you think?' George asked Julian.

Julian thought for a moment but, as he hesitated, Mr Stick appeared from the dungeon entrance, followed by Mrs Stick, who turned to shout back down the steps to Edgar.

'Come on, you lazy, good-for-nothing boy!'

Go to **215**.

229

It was another brilliantly hot and sunny day, and Julian enjoyed his walk. He was turning to have a last look at the wreck, to make sure the Sticks' boat was still there, when he noticed a movement out at sea. At the same time he heard the noise of a powerful engine. He strained his eyes. There was some sort of large motor-vessel out at sea, and it seemed to be heading towards the island.

'I wish I could see it properly,' said Julian to himself. 'I know! I think we brought a pair of binoculars to the island with us. I'll go back to the cave and get them. Oh, *bother* – if I do that the boat will be out of sight by the time I get back.'

He was just about to walk on when he realised the boat had stopped. It was still quite a long way off shore, so he decided to go and get the binoculars for a closer look.

Go to **234.**

230

Each time Julian hit the lock, the trunk shifted a little way. By the time he had hit it seven or eight times, the trunk was only half over the entrance to the dungeons.

'I don't think it's any good leaving the trunk here,' said Dick. 'Every time you hit it, it moves a bit. Anyone coming up from the dungeon and seeing it blocking the entrance would only have to give it a good push to get it out of the way.'

'I think you're right,' said Julian. He stood up.

'What shall we do with it?' asked Dick.

Go to **218.**

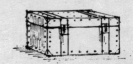

Mr Stick started to push his way into the large bush. Luckily for him it was not a bramble bush, like so many of the other bushes on the cliff-top, but there were plenty of sharp twigs in it, and Mr Stick's hands and arms were soon covered in scratches.

'Here – Edgar,' he said crossly. 'You go back to the dungeons and get my knife for me. Go on, quickly!'

'I'm not going back to no dungeons on my own,' said Edgar. 'There's vicious cows in them dungeons. Something might grab me and I'll never be seen again!'

'Don't be so stupid,' said Mrs Stick. 'There ain't nothing in the dungeons.'

'Well, I'm not going,' said Edgar. 'Not on my own.'

Go to **237.**

Go to **237.**

232

'That's a good idea, Dick,' said George, her eyes shining with glee. 'We can trap those horrible Sticks nicely.'

'You stay here, George,' said Julian, 'Just in case something goes wrong. One of us had better stay hidden.'

George looked sulky for a moment, but she soon realised that Julian was right. If the Sticks should somehow catch Julian and Dick, at least she would still be free, and could even row back to the mainland for help.

Dick and Julian ran down to the courtyard and picked up the trunk. It wasn't quite as heavy as they'd expected. Dick had secretly been imagining that it might be full of gold coins, or bottles of brandy, or diamond necklaces. But he thought any of those would have been much heavier.

They carried the trunk over to the dungeon entrance and set it down.

Go to **235.**

233

If you've arrived from **223**, *score* $\bigcirc\!\!\!\prec \bigcirc\!\!\!\prec$.

Suddenly Anne appeared on the path down from the cliff.

'Where on earth have you all been?' she asked. 'I finished washing up and tidying up the cave ages ago, and I was beginning to wonder if you'd forgotten about me!'

'Oh, no,' said Dick. 'We wouldn't forget about you, but look at all this stuff that the Sticks have brought here from Kirrin Cottage – all sorts of things that belong to Aunt Fanny and Uncle Quentin.'

'Well,' said Julian, 'I think we'd better get everything into the cave. Anne, if you go below again, we can send the things down to you.'

Soon all sorts of things were being lowered into

the cave. The silverware and anything that might be hurt by falling was first wrapped in blankets, then let down by a rope.

Just as they were finishing their job the children heard voices in the distance.

'The Sticks are back!' said Julian.

Go to **219.**

234

He walked back to the cave as quickly as he could, and found Anne there, tidying up the plates they had used for breakfast.

'Hello, Julian,' she said. 'Where are the others?'

'They're still watching the castle,' replied Julian. 'I was following the Sticks when I saw a motor-boat coming towards the island. It's stopped now, so I came down to get the binoculars so that I could have a better look at it. Do you know where they are?'

'Of course I do,' said Anne proudly. She went to the back of the cave and picked up the brown leather case with the binoculars inside it. 'Here you are.'

'Thanks, Anne,' said Julian.

He put the strap of the case around his neck and climbed swiftly up the rope on to the cliff-top. The motor-boat was still there.

Go to **225.**

The trunk covered the mouth of the dungeon entrance quite well, and the two boys were pleased.

'Now, let's see if we can get it open,' said Julian.

'I'm sure it's got smuggled goods in it,' said Dick. 'But it doesn't feel heavy enough for there to be gold coins, does it?'

'No,' said Julian. 'Gold weighs an awful lot. Do your remember how heavy those gold ingots were – the ones we found last year? We could only pick them up one at a time.'

He began to undo the straps. They came undone quite easily, but the trunk was locked, and it was soon clear that the only way Julian could open the locks would be to smash them.

He picked up a large stone and started to bash one of the locks with it.

Go to **230.**

236

George slipped away quietly to warn the others. Before she slid down the rope into the cave, she pulled several bramble sprays across the hole. She dropped down to the floor of the cave and told the other three what had happened.

'We'll be all right here as long as no one falls down that hole in the roof!' said Julian. 'Now keep quiet, everyone, and don't you dare growl, Timmy!'

Nothing was heard for some time, and then Tinker's bark came in the distance.

'Quiet now,' said Julian. 'They're near here.'

The Sticks were up on the cliff once more, searching carefully behind every bush. They came to the great bush behind which the children had hidden, and saw the flattened grass there.

'Someone's been here,' said Mr Stick. 'I wonder if they're in the middle of this bush – it's thick enough to hide an army. I'll try to force my way in, Clara, while you stand by with my gun.'

The children in the cave below held their breath. Would Mr Stick find the hole?

If you think Mr Stick does find the hole, go to **231**.
If you think he doesn't, go to **242**.

237

The children, listening in the cave below, grinned to themselves. They all knew that nothing would make fat, cowardly Edgar go back to the dungeons on his own!

'You'll 'ave to come with me, Ma,' said Edgar.

'Oh, go with him, Clara,' said Mr Stick in exasperation. 'I need that knife to cut through these bushes. You know – that big knife of mine with the very sharp blade.'

Mrs Stick and Edgar disappeared off towards the castle, Mrs Stick still muttering under her breath about Edgar. Mr Stick continued to pull at the bush.

Eventually he decided that there was nothing there.

'I'll just have to look in the other bushes,' he said to himself.

Go to **240**.

238

Edgar opened his eyes and stared around at the four children and their dog in the utmost surprise and horror. He opened his mouth to yell for help but at once found Julian's hand over it.

'Yell just once and Timmy will bite you!' said Julian in a voice as ferocious as Timmy's growl.

'I shan't yell,' said Edgar, speaking in such a low whisper that the others could hardly hear him. 'Keep that dog off. I shan't yell.' He looked at the four of them. 'What're you doing on this island? We thought you'd gone home.'

'It's *our* island,' said George fiercely. 'We've every right to be on it if we want to – but you have no right at all. What are you and your father and mother here for?'

'Don't know,' said Edgar, looking sulky.

'You'd better tell us,' said Julian. 'We know you're in league with smugglers.'

Go to **248**.

Edgar had taken everyone by surprise, and he had a good start on Julian, but Julian was fitter and thinner. Edgar hadn't gone very far before Julian

brought him crashing to the floor of the cave with a flying rugby tackle.

Edgar lay still, all the breath knocked out of him.

'There,' said Julian, as Edgar got up. 'Now don't try that again. You're not getting away from us.'

Go to **244.**

240

Mr Stick walked over to the next clump of brambles and started to pull at it, but the brambles hurt his hands so much that he had to stop. He sat down by the side of the bush to wait for Edgar and Mrs Stick to come back with the knife. As he was sitting there, he put his arms behind him to prop himself up, and one of his hands suddenly disappeared down a hole.

Mr Stick jumped to his feet. 'This cliff is riddled with rabbit holes,' he said to himself. 'Or badger holes, by the size of this one. Best to back off a bit, or I may find the edge giving way.' He moved to what he thought was a safer spot and began to investigate the stump of a tree which stuck out from another clump of brambles.

Down in the cave below, George brushed off the earth that had fallen on her when Mr Stick's hand had suddenly appeared. 'It's all right,' she said to the others. 'You can breathe again. He's gone.'

Meanwhile Mrs Stick and Edgar had got the knife from the dungeons and were walking back to the cliff-top.

'I can't see Dad,' said Edgar. 'He was over there, by that bush. Where on earth has he gone?'

Go to **246.**

241

Once Edgar had been dealt with, Julian turned his attention to the trunk. He got a small rock and tried to smash the two locks. He managed to wrench one open after a while, and then the other gave way too. They all threw back the lid.

On the top was a child's blanket, embroidered with rabbits. Julian pulled it off, expecting to see smuggled goods below. But to his astonishment he found nothing but a little girl's clothes.

He pulled them out. There were two blue jerseys, a blue skirt, some vests and knickers and a warm coat. At the bottom were some dolls and a teddy bear.

'Golly!' said Julian in amazement. 'What are all these for? Why did the Sticks bring these to the island – and why did the smugglers hide them in the wreck?'

George peered into the trunk. 'Is that all?' she asked, prodding at the bottom of the trunk. 'Hold on – I think the base of the trunk is loose. Do you think it might have a false bottom?'

If you think the trunk has a false bottom, go to **247**.
If you think it hasn't, go to **253**.

242

If you've arrived from **246**, *score* ◁ ◁ ◁ ◁.

Edgar wandered off by himself across the cliff. Then, to his horror, he found himself falling! Down he went, and down and down . . . *crash*!

Edgar had fallen down the hole in the roof of the cave. He suddenly appeared before the children's startled eyes. Timmy at once pounced on him with a fearsome growl, but George pulled the dog off.

Edgar was half-stunned with fright and his fall. He lay on the floor of the cave, groaning, his eyes shut. The children stared at him and at one another. For a few moments they were completely taken aback and didn't know what to do or say.

Go to **238.**

243

'Oh look,' said Anne. 'There's something here about the wedding of Princess Elizabeth and Prince Philip.'

'It's very interesting to look at,' said George, 'but it doesn't help us to find out more about what's happening.'

The children sat in silence for a moment, all of them puzzled by the strange contents of the trunk. Just then, the voices of Edgar's parents could be heard shouting for him.

Edgar, who was sitting quietly in a corner of the cave, watched by Timmy, wondered whether he dared shout back.

If Edgar does shout back, go to **258.**
If he decides not to, go to **263.**

244

If you've arrived from **251**, *score* ◁.

Edgar sat on the floor of the cave and glowered at them. 'What are you going to do with me?' he asked. 'My ma and pa will be furious with you if you keep me here.'

His pa and ma were feeling extremely astonished. There had, of course, been nobody hiding
in the bushes on the top of the cliff. And Edgar was
nowhere to be seen.

'Where's that dratted boy?' asked Mr Stick, and
he shouted for him: 'Edgar! *Ed-gar!*'

But Edgar didn't answer. The Sticks spent a
very long time looking for him, both above ground
and under ground. They called and called, but
only the seagulls answered.

Go to **241.**

245

Julian examined the paper carefully. It was difficult to see the date, because the edge of the paper
was rather crumpled and torn, but eventually he
made it out.

'The eleventh of September 1947,' he said. 'I
don't think that can be anything to do with the
Sticks. After all, it was well before any of us were
born!'

They passed the old piece of newspaper around,
looking at the funny advertisements. One of them
was for a pair of gloves, and said that three clothing
coupons were required.

'Clothing coupons!' said Anne in surprise.
'What were they?'

'It was just after the War,' said Julian, 'and
clothes were still rationed. You had to give up so

many coupons for every item of clothing that you bought.'

Go to **243.**

246

'Dad! Dad! Where are you?' shouted Edgar, running up to the cliff-top. In his hurry, Edgar didn't notice that his father was crouched behind the tree stump, digging at the roots with his hands. Edgar ran straight into him from the side. Mr Stick went sprawling into the brambles, and Edgar fell flat on his face!

Mrs Stick came rushing up.

''Ere, Clara, come and get me out of these blasted brambles!' called Mr Stick.

'Get up, Edgar!' ordered his mother. 'You're not hurt.'

'Oh, yes, I am,' said Edgar sulkily. 'My knees are grazed and so are my hands, and I banged my head on this tree stump.'

His mother took absolutely no notice.

'Come and help me get your dad out of them brambles. Quick, now!' she said.

It took a long time to disentangle Mr Stick. Every time one part of him was free, he got caught up somewhere else! Edgar soon lost interest.

Go to **242.**

George's strong fingers felt all around the bottom of the trunk, digging deep into the lining.

'I was right!' she said triumphantly. 'There *is* a false bottom! See if you can help me get it out, Anne. You've got small fingers.'

Anne knelt down beside the trunk and slid her fingers into the lining at the bottom, and together she and George managed to pull the base out.

'Now let's see if there's anything underneath,' said George. 'I bet there is!'

'And I bet there isn't,' said Dick. 'I can't think of anything that would fit in that little space that might be smuggled goods!'

If you think George is right, go to **261.**
If you think Dick is right, go to **253.**

Edgar looked startled. 'Smugglers?' he said. 'I didn't know that. Pa and Ma don't tell me nothing. Now you let me go! You got no right to keep me here.'

'We're not going to let you go,' said George at once. 'If we let you go, you'll go back to your parents and tell them all about us, and we don't want them to know we're here. We're going to spoil their pretty plans, you see.'

Edgar saw. He saw quite a number of things as he looked around the cave at the four children and

Timmy. He stared at the sea through the mouth of the cave, and suddenly he had an idea. Jumping to his feet, he began to run as fast as he could towards the mouth of the cave.

'Hi!' shouted Julian. 'Come back!'

He started to chase after Edgar.

If you think Julian catches Edgar, go to **239.**
If you think he doesn't, go to **254.**

249

They all spent a quiet and rather boring day in the cave. Timmy didn't leave Edgar for a moment. The others discussed their plans in low voices. They decided to keep watch on the cliff-top, two and two together, that night. If the *Roamer* did come, they would make fresh plans then.

The sun sank, and the night came up dark over the sea. They had supper, then Anne and Dick went up to keep the first watch. It was about half-past ten.

At half-past twelve Julian and George joined the other two on the cliff. Dick and Anne had nothing to report, and soon went down into the cave and got into bed.

Julian and George looked out to sea, watching for any sign of a ship. The moon was out now, and things weren't quite so dark. Suddenly they heard low voices and saw shadowy figures on the rocks below.

There was the splash of oars, and the children saw a boat move out over the water.

'The two Sticks,' whispered Julian. 'Going to row out to the wreck again, I suppose.'

At that moment George nudged Julian violently and pointed out to sea. A light was being shown a good way out, from a ship that they could barely see.

'Maybe they're rowing out to that ship over there,' suggested George.

If you think the Sticks are rowing to the wreck, go to **255**.
If you think they are rowing to the other ship, go to **260**.

250

At last the moon sailed out again and lit up the water. They could just make out the shape of the ship, and the Sticks' little boat alongside it.

They watched for a long time before anything happened. Then the little boat began to move away from the side of the ship, and this time it was followed by another rowing-boat.

Go to **257**.

251

'Go on, Timmy, catch him!' said George, her eyes dancing.

Timmy didn't need to be told twice. In a flash he was racing out of cave after Edgar. After a moment they heard a yowling noise, which certainly meant that Timmy had caught Edgar!

The children helped Julian pick himself up, and then they all went out to see what Timmy was doing.

He was standing over Edgar, who was lying flat on the ground on his face, with his arms wrapped around his head. Timmy was holding the back of Edgar's jersey in his mouth, and looking so pleased with himself that all four of them burst out laughing.

'Come on, Timmy,' said George, as soon as she could speak normally. 'You're a very clever dog, but you can leave him alone now!'

'Back into the cave, Edgar!' said Julian.

Go to **244.**

252

If you've arrived from **257**, *score* $\bigcirc$ $\bigcirc$ $\bigcirc$.

After a long time the Sticks' boat reached the shore again, and presently Julian and George could see the Sticks going back towards the castle. Mr Stick carried what looked like a large bundle flung over his shoulder.

The Sticks went into the courtyard of the castle and came to the dungeon entrance. 'They're taking the smuggled goods down there,' Julian whispered to George. 'We'll go back and tell the others, and make more plans. We must somehow or other get those goods ourselves and take them back to the mainland. Then we'll get in touch with the police.'

Suddenly they were startled by a voice calling: 'Help!'

'That sounds like Anne!' said George.

'Oh, do you think so?' said Julian. 'It didn't sound much like her voice. We'd better go and make sure, though.'

If you think it was Anne, go to **259**.
If not, go to **264**.

253

If you've arrived from **247**, *score* ⌒⊲.

George prodded around the bottom of the trunk for a while, but couldn't find anything.

'No, I must have been wrong,' she said regretfully. 'So there are just those children's clothes in the trunk. How very, very strange.'

The children puzzled over it. Clothes seemed such a funny thing to smuggle.

'Well, it beats me,' said Dick at last. 'There's no doubt that peculiar things are afoot here, or the Sticks wouldn't be hanging around our island. And we've seen signals from a ship out at sea. *Something's* going on.'

Just then the voices of Edgar's parents could be heard shouting for him.

Edgar wondered whether he dared shout back.

If you think Edgar does shout back, go to **258**.
If you think he decides not to, go to **263**.

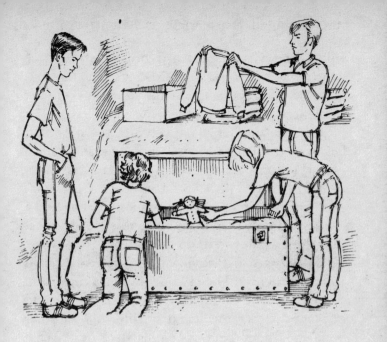

254

Edgar ran madly towards the cave entrance, hotly pursued by Julian. Julian was much fitter and lighter on his feet than Edgar, who was fat and out of condition, but Edgar had a good start. As Julian sped after him, however, he caught his foot on the edge of one of the cushions and went sprawling!

Edgar took a swift backward look and, seeing Julian spread out on the floor of the cave, he ran even faster. A moment or two later he was out of the cave. Dick had begun to go after him, but George had a better idea.

Go to **251.**

Julian and George watched breathlessly to see which way the Sticks were rowing. Was the shadowy ship a good way out the *Roamer*? Were the smugglers at work tonight?

'There's another boat coming – look!' said George. 'It must have come from that ship out to sea. It's going to the old wreck. It must be a meeting-place.'

Then, most irritatingly, the moon went behind a cloud, and remained there for some time. At last it sailed out again and lit up the water.

'Both boats are leaving the wreck now,' said Julian excitedly. 'They've had their meeting – and passed over the smuggled goods, I suppose – and now one boat is returning to the ship, and the other boat, the Sticks' boat, is coming back here. We'll follow the Sticks when they get back and see where they put the goods.'

Go to **252.**

Julian walked over to Dick's bed and pulled back the blankets. Dick wasn't there!

'Where on earth can he have gone?' said George, sounding very startled. 'We didn't see him while we were out on the cliff-top. I hope he's all right.'

'Perhaps we'd better go and look for him,' suggested Anne.

'I don't suppose he's very far away,' said Julian. 'After all, this is a small island and there aren't many places where he *could* be!'

'Yes, but maybe the Sticks have captured him,' said George. 'Perhaps he woke up and decided to do some exploring on his own, and the Sticks found him and took him down to the dungeons!'

Julian thought it over.

'I'm afraid that might be what happened,' he said at last. 'I think we'd better go over to the castle and see if we can find out. George, you come with me. Anne, you stay here with Timmy and keep an eye on Edgar.'

Go to **262.**

257

The two small boats moved smoothly over the water towards the old wreck.

'They're both heading for the wreck,' George hissed to Julian. 'What on *earth* can they be doing?'

'I can't think,' said Julian. 'But it's all very odd.'

They watched in silence as the two boats reached the wreck. They could just catch the sound of voices, but couldn't hear what was being said. There was another long wait while nothing happened, and George almost went to sleep! Then suddenly Julian spoke.

'Both boats are leaving the wreck,' he said excitedly. 'They've had their meeting – and passed over the smuggled goods, I suppose – and now one boat is returning to the ship, and the other, the Sticks' boat, is coming back here. We'll follow the Sticks when they get back and see where they put the goods.'

Go to **252.**

258

If you've arrived from **268**, *score* ◯ ◯.
If you've arrived from **243**, *score* ◯ ◯ ◯.

Edgar looked at the children, who were still examining the clothes from the trunk. He decided to risk shouting, hoping that his parents would hear him. 'Help!' he yelled.

The word was hardly out of his mouth when Timmy nipped his ankle. It was only a tiny bite, and didn't even break the skin, but Edgar gave a howl of pain. Dick leapt across the cave and put his hand over Edgar's mouth.

'Shut up!' Dick hissed fiercely. 'If you yell again we'll let Timmy do anything he wants to, and you won't like it! Now, when I take my hand away you keep quiet, or else. Understand?'

Edgar nodded his head, and Dick took his hand away.

Immediately Edgar opened his mouth to tell the children what he thought of them, but Timmy gave a low, fierce growl and bared his teeth.

'Timmy, you stay right beside Edgar, and if he shouts you nip his leg!' ordered George.

Go to **263.**

George and Julian slid down the rope into the cave, and an astonishing sight met their eyes. Timmy and Edgar were rolling over and over in the middle of the floor! Timmy was making a ferocious noise, and Edgar was trying to get his breath to yell. However, he was struggling so hard with Timmy that he couldn't manage to speak at all.

Anne was sitting up in bed looking very worried.

'Oh, there you are,' she said in relief as Julian and George dropped down into the cave.

'Whatever is going on, Anne?' asked George.

Go to **267.**

260

Julian and George watched breathlessly to see which way the Sticks were rowing. They seemed to be heading towards the wreck, but it was difficult to see them clearly, as the moon kept sliding in and out behind clouds.

'They're not making very much noise,' said Julian. 'I can only just hear the sound of the oars. You'd think that on a still night like this we'd hear every stroke they make.'

'I expect they've muffled the oars to make less noise,' said George. 'You know – they tie some cloth around the oars so that they don't make a splash each time they hit the water.'

They watched the small boat moving over the water for a minute, then George said quietly:

'They're not going to the wreck. They're too far out from the rocks for that. They must be rowing out to that ship that's showing a light, much further out. I wonder if that ship is the *Roamer*?'

Go to **265.**

261

George peered into the trunk.

'There *is* something down here!' she exclaimed in excitement. 'Hold on a moment while I pull it out. It's caught in the side of the trunk.'

'Here, let me see if I can get it out,' said Anne. 'Oh, it's a piece of newspaper, that's all.'

Julian and Dick looked disappointed. If all that was under the false bottom of the trunk was an old newspaper, then it wasn't likely to help them very much!

Anne worked the paper loose and held it up triumphantly.

'Let me have a look at that, Anne,' said Julian, taking the paper from his sister. 'Now – I wonder what the date on this is?'

'Why does it matter what the date on the newspaper is?' asked Dick.

'Well,' said Julian, 'if it's an old newspaper, the chances are that it won't have anything to do with what's going on here on Kirrin Island, but if it's a recent paper it may give us a clue.'

If you think the paper is a recent one, go to **268.**
If you think it's an old one, go to **245.**

Julian and George climbed up the rope on to the cliff-top and set off towards the castle. Just as they reached a point where they could see down into the courtyard, Dick came walking towards them!

'Where have you been?' demanded George. 'We thought the Sticks had got you in the dungeons!'

'Oh, no,' said Dick cheerfully, 'I wouldn't let that happen to me. I thought I heard the noise of a power-boat coming to the island, so I decided to get up and have a look, but there was nothing there.'

Julian explained to Dick about Edgar and Timmy fighting, and Anne not being able to stop Timmy.

'I expect Edgar was trying to run away,' he finished, 'and Timmy was stopping him. Come on, I think we'd better go back to the cave and tell Anne you're all right.'

Just then the three children were startled by a scream. It was high-pitched and sounded terrified.

Go to **266.**

263

If you've arrived from **258**, *score* ◌.
If you've arrived from **268**, *score* ◌ ◌.
If you've arrived from **243**, *score* ◌ ◌ ◌.

Timmy's nose was poked against Edgar's legs, so that he could nip Edgar at any time. Edgar decided to keep quiet.

'Do you know anything about the ship that signals to this island at night?' asked Julian, turning to Edgar.

The boy shook his head. 'Never heard of no signals,' he said. 'I just heard my mother saying that she expected the *Roamer* tonight, but I don't know what she meant.'

'The *Roamer*?' said George at once. 'What's that – a man – or a boat – or what?'

'I don't know,' said Edgar. 'I'd only have got a clip on the ear if I'd asked. Find out for yourselves.'

'We shall,' said Julian grimly. 'Thanks for the information.'

Go to **249.**

264

They got up and started to walk back to the hole down to the cave. Just as they got there, they heard another cry. It was a real scream this time, high-pitched and terrified. It frightened George and Julian very much.

They both slid rapidly down the rope into the cave. Anne was peacefully asleep in her bed, and so was Dick. Edgar still snored, and Timmy watched, his eyes gleaming green.

'Funny,' said Julian. '*Very* funny. Who screamed like that? It couldn't possibly have been Anne – because if she had screamed in her sleep like that she would have woken the others.'

'Well, who screamed then?' said George, feeling rather scared. 'Wasn't it weird, Julian?'

They woke Dick and Anne and told them about the strange scream and all the things they had seen that night.

Go to **270.**

265

The Sticks rowed steadily on towards the faint light out at sea. Julian and George stared intently. Was the shadowy ship the *Roamer*? Or was the owner of it 'the Roamer'? Were the smugglers at work tonight?

Then, most irritatingly, the moon went behind a cloud again and remained there for some time.

Go to **250.**

266

'Do you suppose that's Anne again?' said George.

'We'd better go and see,' said Dick, and they all rushed back to the cave.

Anne was sleeping peacefully when they got back and Edgar was snoring. Only Timmy was awake, his ears pricked up for any sound.

They woke Anne and told her about the scream, and the four children discussed the night's events in low voices.

Go to **270.**

George called to Timmy. 'Here, boy!'

Timmy gave a last regretful look at Edgar, who was now lying flat on his back in the middle of the cave with his eyes closed, and trotted obediently over to George.

'What happened, Anne?' asked George again.

'Well, I woke up and found Timmy and Edgar having a fight,' said Anne. 'I called to Timmy to try to make him stop, but he took no notice of me. I was afraid that he might really hurt Edgar, so I decided to shout for help.'

'Why didn't you wake Dick?' asked Julian. 'He would have helped you.'

'I tried to wake him,' replied Anne, 'but he didn't answer. He's a terribly heavy sleeper, you know.'

Julian looked over at the hump of bedclothes on Dick's side of the cave.

'You know, I don't think he's there!' said Julian.

'Don't be silly,' said George. 'Where could he be except in bed?'

If you think Dick is in bed, go to **273**.
If you think he isn't, go to **256**.

Julian looked at the top of the newspaper.

'The seventh!' he exclaimed. 'That's only a week ago. And look, there's an item here that someone has drawn a ring around. I wonder why?'

'What's it about, Julian?' asked Dick. 'Is it about Kirrin Island, or smugglers, or something like that?'

'No,' said Julian. 'It's about a millionaire called Harry Armstrong buying a big new house by the sea not very far from here. I can't imagine why anybody should be particularly interested in that, can you?'

The children sat in silence for a moment, all of them puzzled by the strange contents of the trunk. Just then, the voices of Edgar's parents could be heard shouting for him.

Edgar, who was sitting quietly in a corner of the cave, watched by Timmy, wondered whether he dared shout back.

If Edgar does shout back, go to **258.**
If he decides not to, go to **263.**

269

It was much more difficult walking in the dark than they had imagined it would be. There was very little moonlight, and the paths that were so familiar and easy in daylight looked quite different at night.

All of a sudden Dick caught his foot on something and tripped. He wasn't hurt, and soon picked himself up again, but before they'd gone very much further George caught her foot in a rabbit hole and went sprawling. She tried to get to her feet but sank back with an exclamation of pain.

'What's the matter,' asked Anne.

'I've twisted my ankle a bit,' answered George. 'It's rather painful.'

'Can you walk on it?' asked Julian.

George sat and rubbed her ankle hard for a minute or two, then tried to put some weight on it.

'Yes, I can walk on it,' she said, 'but I don't think I'll be able to run, and that might be a problem when we get down into the dungeons.'

'I think we'd better go back to the cave,' said Julian. 'Dick's fallen over, and you've hurt your ankle. I don't think it would be sensible to go on any further.'

So they turned back to the cave, and it wasn't long before they were ready for bed.

'Oh, Julian,' said Anne, 'I can't help thinking about that poor girl. We *must* rescue her!'

Go to **276.**

270

If you've arrived from **278**, *score* ◁ ◁ ◁.
If you've arrived from **266**, *score* ◁ ◁ ◁ ◁.

'Do you think it was a girl's scream?' asked Anne.

'Yes. It sounded like the scream you give when one of us jumps out at you suddenly,' replied Julian. 'A proper little girl's scream, not a yell like a boy would give.' He looked at the others. 'A little girl,' he said slowly. 'We thought we heard a girl scream tonight, and the trunk was full of girls' clothes and dolls. What does it mean?'

208

There was silence, then Anne spoke excitedly.

'I know! The smuggled goods are a little girl! The clothes and dolls are for her to wear and play with. And you heard her scream when the Sticks carried her down into the dungeons!'

'I do believe Anne has hit on the answer,' said Julian. 'It isn't smugglers who are using the island, it's kidnappers! The Sticks will keep her here until a large sum of money has been paid for her release.'

'Julian, we've got to rescue her!' said George. 'Let's go now.'

'Hadn't we better wait until morning?' suggested Dick.

If you think they should try to rescue the girl immediately, go to **281.**
If you think they should wait until morning, go to **276.**

271

Julian thought for a moment or two. Then he decided to go down into the dungeons straight away. After all, the Sticks might come back sooner than he expected, and he badly wanted to get the little girl out of her dungeon as soon as he could. She must be very frightened, alone down there in the dark.

He ran quickly down into the courtyard of the castle. There were one or two tin cans lying around, and some crisp packets. Obviously the Sticks had had their supper in the courtyard last night and hadn't bothered to clear up properly.

Beasts! thought Julian. They might at least pick up their horrible litter instead of leaving it around our castle.

He walked towards the dungeon entrance, and then paused. Lying on the stones just in front of him, fast asleep, was Tinker. His back was towards Julian, and Julian stood still. Could he sneak past without Tinker noticing him, or would the dog wake up and chase him?

If you think he can get past Tinker, go to **286.**
If you think Tinker will wake up, go to **280.**

272

'Anne, you know where everything is in here. Can you find a couple of spare torches?' asked Julian.

'Do you think we ought to take torches?' said Dick. 'If either of the Sticks comes out of the cave, they'll see the light of a torch straight away.'

'That's a good point,' said George. 'We'll have to do without. After all, we know this island pretty well, and there's some moonlight tonight.'

'We'll just have to watch our steps,' said Julian. 'Come on, then, let's go.'

One by one they clambered up the rope, then the four of them picked their way towards the castle.

Go to **269.**

Julian walked over to Dick's bed and pulled back the blankets. Dick was curled up right at the bottom, his pillow pulled over his head! Julian started to laugh.

'No wonder he couldn't hear you, Anne,' he said. 'Come on, Dick, wake up. We've got things to tell you!'

Dick sat up, rubbing his eyes. 'W . . . what's going on?' he said sleepily. 'Why is Edgar lying in the middle of the floor?'

They had all forgotten Edgar, who was still lying with his eyes shut.

'He was trying to run away, I think,' said Anne, 'and Timmy went after him and tried to stop him. It was their fighting that woke me up.'

Julian walked over to Edgar and pulled him to his feet.

'Now, you get back to your corner and stay there,' he ordered. 'Don't try to escape again, or it'll be the worse for you, won't it, Timmy?'

Timmy growled at Edgar, who slunk into a corner and sat down.

Go to **278.**

Go to **278.**

274

The four of them went back into the cave.

'Come with us, Edgar,' said Julian. 'You too, Timmy.'

Edgar was very reluctant, but in the end he climbed up the rope out of the cave, with Timmy snapping at his heels. Timmy then ran out of the cave mouth and raced round to join the others up on the cliff.

'Right, quick march!' said Julian, who wanted to get everything over before the Sticks came back. And quick march it was, across the cliffs, over the low wall of the castle and down into the courtyard. Tinker was still there, lying asleep in the sunshine. He sat up as the children approached, and saw Timmy. Tinker immediately launched himself at Timmy, barking at the top of his voice. Timmy was quite happy to have the chance to fight his old enemy, and the two dogs rolled over and over in

the middle of the courtyard, biting and growling.

'Timmy!' shouted George. 'Leave Tinker alone!'

For once Timmy took no notice of George. He was enjoying himself too much.

Julian, Dick and George had forgotten Edgar, and now he began to edge slowly away from the others. Suddenly he took to his heels and ran out of the courtyard.

'Edgar!' shouted Julian. 'You come back here!'

But Edgar took no notice.

'We'd better go after him, I suppose,' said Dick.

'I think we'd better go down and rescue the little girl first,' said George. 'After all, he can't get off the island.'

'No, but he might go back to the cave and frighten Anne,' said Dick.

If you think they should go after Edgar, go to **296.**
If you think they should go down to the dungeons, go to **287.**

275

The bright light in the cave dazzled their eyes after the darkness of the tunnels, so they didn't see Edgar straight away. He was over at the mouth of the cave, looking out to see if there were any sign of his mother and father coming back from the mainland, but the only vessel to be seen was a trawler, chugging lazily towards the open sea.

'Hey, Edgar!' shouted Julian. 'Come here!'

Edgar turned around and saw Julian, George and Timmy standing at the mouth of the tunnel. He stared wildly around the cave. Should he just give himself up? Should he run out of the cave on to the beach, and see if he could get away across the rocks? Or should he try to find another way out of the cave?

If you think he gives himself up, go to **289.**
If you think he escapes through the mouth of the cave, go to **290.**
If you think he tries to find another way out of the cave, go to **293.**

276

If you've arrived from **269,** *score* ◁ ◁ ◁.

'We'll rescue her, never fear,' said Julian. 'But let's wait until tomorrow.'

They all lay down and went to sleep, rather tired after the night's events. Timmy lay with one eye open all night long, on guard.

Next day Julian woke early and went up the rope to the cliff to see if the Sticks were about. He saw them coming up the steps from the dungeons. Mrs Stick looked pale and worried.

'We've got to find our Edgar,' she kept saying to Mr Stick.

'Well, he's not on the island,' replied Mr Stick. 'We hunted all over it yesterday. I think whoever was on the island then took our belongings, caught

Edgar, and made off with him and everything else in their boat.'

'We'd better go back to the mainland and ask a few questions,' said Mrs Stick. 'They're bound to have taken him back there.'

'What about Tinker?' asked Mr Stick. 'We'd better leave him here, to guard the entrance to the dungeons, hadn't we? Not that there's anyone here, if what you say is right.'

They left Tinker in the courtyard, and Julian saw them go down to the cove and get into their boat. He hesitated, trying to decide whether to go down into the dungeons straight away or to go back and tell the others.

If you think he should go down into the dungeons, go to **271.**

If you think he should go back and tell the others, go to **283.**

277

If you've arrived from **288**, *score* ◁ ◁.
If you've arrived from **295**, *score* ◁ ◁ ◁.

They all turned their torches on. There was no need to worry about anyone seeing the light this time, as they knew the Sticks weren't down there. They made their way towards the dungeon with the wooden door, moving in single file down the passage. Suddenly Julian, who was walking just in front of Edgar, stumbled and dropped his torch.

'Oh, bother!' exclaimed Julian. 'Hang on a minute. I must find my torch. George, can you shine your torch on to the ground so I can look?'

George did as Julian asked, and Dick joined in the search. Nobody thought about Edgar, who for once in his life had used his head. Julian's torch had fallen against his foot and, in the confusion while the others were looking for it, Edgar had picked it up. Suddenly he took to his heels and ran off down the passage.

'Quick!' shouted Dick. 'Old Spotty-Face is running away!'

The three of them rushed after Edgar, but he had a good start. When they reached a point where the passages divided, they had no idea which way he had gone.

'I'll search this passage,' said Dick, pointing to one that led off to the left.

'Then I'd better go with George,' said Julian, 'since I've got no torch. Come on – let's take this passage to the right.'

If you want to follow Dick, go to **292.**
If you want to follow Julian and George, go to **282.**

278

'If everything is all right,' said Julian, 'I think George and I should go back on watch again, in case anything else happens tonight. You go back to sleep for a while.'

Dick and Anne got back into bed, and the other two swarmed up the rope to the cliff-top.

'Let's walk over to the castle and see if the Sticks are about,' suggested George.

They had only gone a few steps when they were startled by a piercing scream. It was high-pitched and terrified.

'Do you think Edgar's trying to escape again?' said George.

Julian shook his head. 'I don't suppose so,' he said. 'But I think we'd better go back and tell the others what we've heard. Come on.'

Dick and Anne were still awake, but they hadn't heard anything. Edgar had gone back to sleep and was snoring peacefully. The four children discussed the night's events in low voices.

Go to **270.**

279

Julian walked back up the cliff to start looking for Edgar. He looked in every possible hiding-place as he went, but it was such a small island that it didn't take him very long to go all round it. There was no sign of Edgar anywhere, so Julian thought he would go back to the cave to see if by any chance Edgar had gone there.

He walked over to the hole in the cliff and slid down the rope into the cave.

Go to **298.**

Julian took a few cautious steps past Tinker, moving as quietly as he could, but it was no good. Tinker opened his eyes, sat up, and saw Julian. He gave an enormous yelp and flew at Julian, worrying at his ankles and making Julian dance up and down!

'Go away, Stinker!' ordered Julian. 'Go away!'

But Tinker was not as well trained as Timmy, and he continued to nip at poor Julian's legs. Julian gave up and beat a hasty retreat back to the cliff. He sat down, rubbing his ankles with his handkerchief. Tinker's bites had made his ankles bleed in one or two places. He thought things over for a while then got to his feet.

Go to **283.**

'Let's go now,' repeated George. 'That poor girl must be so scared down there with the Sticks! We must rescue her tonight.'

Edgar woke up and joined in the conversation.

'What are you talking about?' he asked. 'Rescue who?'

'Never you mind,' said Julian. 'Right, we'll go tonight, but we'll have to do something about old Spotty-Face over there.'

'Timmy will guard him, won't you, boy?' said George.

The dog gave an eager *'Woof'* and planted himself right in front of Edgar, who sat propped against the side of the cave, looking very sulky, as the others made their plans.

Go to **272.**

282

Julian, George and Timmy ran down the passage, hoping to see the light from Edgar's torch bobbing in front of them. Soon the floor of the passage started to slope downwards, very steeply. They had to slow down to a walk, picking their way carefully so as not to fall over the rocks that studded the passage floor.

'I wonder where on earth we're going to end up?' said George. 'If this passage is leading to another dungeon, it must be a very long way under the ground!'

Gradually the slope of the passage grew less steep, and then a glimmer of light appeared, and next minute they had emerged into a cave.

'Perhaps Edgar's hiding in here,' suggested George.

If you think Edgar is in the cave, go to **275.**
If you think he isn't there, go to **305.**

If you've arrived from **280**, *score* ⌒⌒ .
If you've arrived from **291**, *score* ⌒⌒⌒ .

Julian decided to go back and tell the others what had happened, so he returned to the cave and dropped down the rope, startling Edgar very much.

'Come outside the cave and I'll tell you my plans,' he said to the others. He didn't want Edgar to hear them. 'Listen!' he said, when they were all outside. 'The Sticks have gone off in their boat back to the mainland to see if they can find Edgar. I propose that we go down to the dungeons now and rescue the girl. Then we bring her back to the cave for some breakfast. After that we can take her back to the mainland in our boat. We'll go to the police, and they'll find her parents. As for Edgar, we can put him in the dungeons instead of the girl!'

'*What* a good idea!' said Anne, and all the others laughed and agreed.

'You stay here, Anne, and make some breakfast for us all,' said Julian. He knew that Anne hated going down into the dungeons.

Go to **274**.

Julian looked towards the cave, where Edgar was making for the tunnel back to the dungeons.

'You go and find Timmy,' he told George, 'and I'll see if I can catch old Spotty-Face.'

George started to scramble back over the rocks, calling Timmy's name and whistling. Suddenly she heard a whimper, so she stood still and listened. She heard it again. It seemed to be coming from the right, so she started to search among the rocks. Supposing Timmy had fallen and hurt himself?

Go to **302.**

285

Julian disappeared beyond the castle walls, and Dick and George began to search the castle. There weren't very many places where Edgar could hide, and it wasn't long before they found him, in a corner of the little room with the collapsed roof, crouching behind a pile of rubble.

'All right, out you come,' said Dick, grabbing Edgar's arm. 'You're not getting away from us that easily!'

Edgar stumbled out into the courtyard and sat down on a rock.

'One of us had better go and tell Julian that we've found Edgar,' said Dick. 'We don't want to waste any more time in getting down into the dungeons. Shall I go, George, and you and Timmy stay here and keep an eye on old Spotty-Face?'

George nodded. 'That's a good idea,' she said.

'Edgar won't try to get away again as long as Timmy is keeping an eye on him!'

Go to **288.**

286

Julian took a few cautious steps past Tinker, moving as quietly as he could. Tinker continued to sleep peacefully, and Julian breathed a sigh of relief as he trod warily towards the dungeon entrance. But suddenly Tinker sprang to his feet and started to bark. Julian turned around to see if the dog was chasing him, but to his surprise Tinker was running towards the cove. At the same moment Julian heard voices. The Sticks were coming back!

He didn't have time to get out of the castle and run back to the cave, so he looked around for a hiding-place. There was no time to get down into the dungeons, but he remembered the little room where the roof had fallen in. If he could hide in there, behind one of the piles of stones, he would probably be all right. He dashed into the little room and squeezed himself behind some of the rubble just as the Sticks walked into the courtyard.

Go to **291.**

287

'Let's go down to the dungeons,' said Julian. 'We may not have much time. I don't think Edgar will go back to the cave – he's more likely to try to hide somewhere.'

Just then Timmy, giving Tinker a last shake, looked up and saw Edgar disappearing into the distance. He tore after him, and a moment or two later a cross-looking Edgar appeared, with Timmy close behind growling softly.

'Well done, Timmy!' said George, giving him a pat. 'Don't try that again, Edgar, or you'll be sorry!'

'Let's get these stones off the dungeon entrance,' said Julian. 'Come on, Edgar, you can give us a hand.'

Edgar pulled with the rest, and one by one the rocks were moved away. Then the heavy trapdoor stone was hauled up too, and the flight of steps was exposed, leading down into darkness.

Go to **277.**

288

Dick went away across the courtyard and up on to the cliffs. He hadn't walked very far when he saw Julian coming towards him.

'Hey, Julian!' Dick called. 'We've found Edgar. We can go down to the dungeons now.'

'Where was he hiding?' asked Julian.

'Oh, behind a pile of rubble in that little room where the roof's fallen in,' replied Dick. 'He didn't get very far!'

'Right,' said Julian when they were all back in

the castle, 'let's move those stones. Come on, Edgar, you can help us.'

Edgar pulled with the rest, and one by one the rocks were moved away. Then the heavy trapdoor stone was hauled up too, and the flight of steps was exposed, leading down into darkness.

Go to **277.**

289

Edgar stood still for a moment, wondering what to do.

'Come here, Edgar,' ordered Julian, 'or we'll send Timmy to get you!'

The last thing Edgar wanted was another encounter with Timmy's teeth, so he shambled back across the cave to where Julian and George were waiting.

'Right,' said Julian. 'We're going back to the dungeon with the wooden door now. You can go first, George, then Edgar, then me, and Timmy can walk just behind Edgar in case he tries to run away again. You can give me back my torch, too, Edgar!'

As the three children and Timmy began to make their way along the steeply sloping tunnel, Edgar suddenly kicked Timmy hard on one of his back legs. Timmy yelped in pain. Then Edgar gave George a shove, which sent her flying, and raced off down the passage.

'Come back, you beast!' yelled Julian, but Edgar was already out of sight. Julian bent over George, who was rolling around on the ground, clutching her leg.

'Are you all right, George?' he asked.

'I'll be fine in a minute,' said George. 'I banged my knee rather hard when Edgar shoved me.' Timmy looked very worried, and kept nudging her with his nose.

Julian gave George's leg a good rub, then she got to her feet and they set off after Edgar. He had a good start by this time, and in the end Julian and George realised that they couldn't find him in the maze of tunnels and dungeons. They made their way back to the dungeon with the wooden door to wait for Dick.

It wasn't very long before he appeared, dragging a sulky Edgar with him.

'Well done, Dick! He got away from us, the little horror,' said Julian.

George put Timmy to stand guard over Edgar. Timmy, remembering the kick, growled menacingly.

Go to **306.**

290

Edgar decided to try to get away across the rocks outside the cave. Luckily for him the tide was out, and he started to scramble over the slippery rocks. Julian, George and Timmy ran after him, but he had a good start.

Edgar hadn't gone very far when he came to a place where the rocks rose sharply and smoothly up to the cliffs. He couldn't go any further, so he turned and made his way out towards the sea for a short while, then doubled back, hoping to get to the cave before the others could reach him.

Just then Edgar had a stroke of luck. Julian slipped and fell, and while George stopped to help him, Edgar sneaked back into the cave.

George looked around to see if Timmy was chasing Edgar.

'Julian,' she said. 'Timmy – he's not here!'

Go to **284.**

291

Julian could hear the Sticks arguing crossly.

'I thought you'd have had the sense to bring some money with you, Clara,' said Mr Stick. ''Ow did you think we were going to manage without any cash?'

'Why does it always be me who has to have money?' said Mrs Stick. 'Why can't you provide some cash for a change?'

'Well, help me move the stones from the dungeon entrance, and I'll get some money from my jacket,' said Mr Stick.

Julian heard nothing for about ten minutes, and he guessed that the Sticks were down in the dungeons. Then he heard their voices again.

'Come on, Clara, hurry up. Let's get back to Kirrin as quick as we can,' said Mr Stick. 'We've wasted enough time as it is.'

Their voices died away. Julian counted to a

hundred, slowly, before he moved cautiously out of the little room. He looked out to sea. The Stick's boat was moving steadily over the water towards the mainland.

Go to **283.**

292

The passage was wide and smooth, obviously worn by many feet. As Dick ran down it, he paused to listen for the sound of footsteps, but he couldn't hear anything. After some time he came to a side passage on the right hand side and turned into it, shining his torch in front of him. Eventually he came to a place where the passage divided, and he decided to turn left.

As he walked along the passage it seemed to be bending further round to the left. Suddenly the light of a torch flashed past in front of him, and he heard the sound of running footsteps. Was it Edgar? Dick ran to the end of the passage and turned right. He was back in the wide passage.

He grinned to himself. He remembered exploring this tunnel last summer, and he knew that it came to a dead end! At the end of it was a bottle dungeon, empty at low tide, but which filled with water when the tide came in. Any prisoner put in there would drown. Edgar would have to turn back, and Dick could catch him then. He slowed to a walk. There was no need to run after Edgar when he couldn't get away.

Go to **297.**

Edgar stared around the cave, looking for a way of escape. He obviously couldn't get past Julian and George and into the tunnel, and he didn't like the idea of trying to scramble over the rocks. Then suddenly he saw what looked like the entrance to another tunnel. He dashed across the cave and vanished into it just as Timmy came bounding after him.

'Timmy! Come back!' called George. She didn't want Timmy disappearing in case he got lost. Timmy trotted back to George rather reluctantly. He would have enjoyed chasing Edgar!

'I wonder where he's vanished to?' said Julian. 'He disappeared behind that pile of rocks. We'd better have a closer look at it.'

Go to **303.**

294

Dick went to the little girl and put his arm around her. 'Everything's all right now,' he said. 'You're safe.'

Tears ran down the girl's cheeks again. 'Why am I here? I don't like being here!'

'Oh, it's just an adventure you've had,' said Julian. 'It's nearly over now, and you can have breakfast with us in our lovely cave.'

'What's your name?' asked George.

'Jennifer Mary Armstrong,' said the girl. 'What are you all called?'

They told her their names, and then Jennifer looked at Edgar.

'Who is he?' she asked.

'Edgar is the son of the people who put you in here,' replied Julian. 'We're going to leave him here in your place, as a surprise for his parents when they get back.'

Dick brought Jennifer out into the passage, then Julian pushed Edgar into the cave and slammed the door. They could hear him howling as they made their way back to the entrance.

Jennifer breathed in great gulps of fresh, sea-smelling air.

'Oh, this is lovely!' she said. 'Where am I?'

'On our island,' said George, 'and this is our ruined castle.'

229

'Sh-ssh!' said Dick suddenly. 'I thought I heard a noise coming from the little room.'

The children all stood still.

'Do you think we should investigate?' said Dick, 'or should we get Jennifer back to the cave?'

If you think they should investigate, go to **308.**
If you think they should go straight back to the cave, go to **301.**

295

Anne gave him a packet of biscuits, and he went back to where Dick and George were still waiting for him. He was glad to see that they had found Edgar.

'Where was he?' asked Julian.

'Oh, behind a pile of rubble in the little room,' replied Dick. 'He didn't get very far!'

'Right, Spotty-Face,' said Julian. 'You can come and help us get the stones off the dungeon entrance.'

Edgar gave a hand with the rest, and one by one the rocks were moved away. Then the heavy trap-door stone was hauled up too, and the flight of steps was exposed, leading down into darkness.

Go to **277.**

296

'I think we'd better go after him,' said Julian. 'We don't want him going back to the cave.'

By this time Edgar had vanished.

'Oh, blow!' said George. 'Old spotty-face Edgar could be anywhere by now. 'We'd better split up and look for him.'

'You and Dick search round in here,' said Julian, 'and I'll go outside the castle and look around the rest of the island.'

If you want to stay with Dick and George, go to **285**.
If you want to follow Julian, go to **279**.

297

Sure enough, after a minute or two Dick saw the light of Edgar's torch coming back along the tunnel. Dick shone his torch at Edgar to dazzle him, and as Edgar put up his arm to shield his eyes, Dick grabbed it.

'Right, Spotty-Face,' he said. 'You come back to the others now! Don't try to run away again, either, or else.'

Dick marched Edgar back to the dungeon with the wooden door, where the others, who had given up their search, were waiting.

Go to **306**.

298

Anne was busy preparing breakfast. She had set out five plates – one for each of them – and one for the little girl.

'Are you all right?' Julian asked her.

'Yes, thank you, I'm fine,' replied Anne. 'Why have you come back? Is anything wrong?'

Julian didn't want to worry her by telling her that Edgar had escaped. 'I just came to fetch some biscuits,' he said. 'Old Spotty-Face will need something to eat when we lock him in the dungeon.'

Go to **295.**

299

'Hey, George!' called a voice.

George looked up and saw Julian coming towards her across the rocks.

'I see you've found Timmy all right,' went on Julian. 'Where was he?'

'He'd fallen into a rock pool and couldn't get out,' replied George. 'Did you catch old Spotty-Face?'

'No, I couldn't find him,' replied Julian. 'He could be anywhere now. You know what a maze all those tunnels are.'

The three of them made their way back to the dungeon with the wooden door to wait for Dick, and it wasn't very long before he appeared, dragging a sulky Edgar with him.'

'Well done, Dick! He got away from us, the little horror,' said Julian.

George put Timmy to stand guard over Edgar.

Go to **306.**

Julian, who was in front of George, stopped suddenly with a startled: 'Ouch!'

'What's the matter, Julian?' asked George. 'Have you hurt yourself?'

Julian didn't answer, but George could hear odd scuffling noises and muffled grunts and groans.

'Julian! What's going on?' asked George again, but Julian still didn't answer. Shining her torch as far in front of her as she could, George could just see Julian's legs kicking and struggling.

'George!' shouted Julian. 'I'm stuck in this narrow bit of the tunnel, and I can't move either way!'

George started to laugh. It was so funny to think of Julian stuck like that.

'I coiled a rope round my waist in case we needed it,' he explained, 'and it's made me too wide to get through this narrow bit of the tunnel.'

'How are you going to get out, then?' asked George. 'Any ideas?'

Go to **307**.

301

If you've arrived from **304**, *score* ◁ ◁.

They hesitated, wondering what to do. Then suddenly Tinker appeared and made a rush at Timmy.

'Oh, that beastly dog!' said George. 'Let's get away from him, back to the cave. He always upsets Timmy.'

They returned to the cave, where Anne made Jennifer welcome. They were all very hungry and ate a large breakfast while Jennifer told them about herself.

'I was playing in the garden one day when a man suddenly climbed over the wall, threw a shawl over my head and took me away. We live by the sea, you know, and I soon realised that I was in a boat, rocking on the waves. I was taken to a big ship and locked in a cabin for two days, and then I was brought here.'

'I think we'd better take you back to the mainland straight away,' said Julian. 'We'll take you to the police station, Jennifer. I'm sure they're looking for you!'

Go to **309.**

302

'Timmy! Timmy! Where are you?' George called.

There was an answering bark, and, looking over the edge of a spur of rock, George saw Timmy below her. He was standing in a rock pool, obviously unhurt, and wagging his tail with pleasure at seeing her. George could tell at a glance that he wouldn't be able to get out of the pool without help, because the sides were very smooth and slippery. Looking around, she saw that the far edge of the pool was lower than the piece she was standing on, so she moved over there and lay down on her stomach on the rocks. She stretched both arms down and took hold of Timmy's front legs, pulling them up so that he was standing on his back legs.

'Now Timmy, jump!' she said.

Timmy gave a spring, George pulled hard, and the dog landed in a heap on top of her, safe and sound.

George got to her feet and gave herself a shake.

'Goodness, you're wet, Timmy! I'm soaked!' she said. 'Let's go and find Julian, shall we? I wonder if he's caught up with Edgar yet?'

Go to **299.**

303

If you've arrived from **293**, *score* ◠ꞁ.

'Oh look,' said George. 'Here's another passage! Edgar must have gone up here. Come on, Julian!'

They started to explore, Julian going first. It was narrow at the beginning, but soon widened out so that they could walk upright. The air felt damp, and there was a strong smell of the sea.

'I should think the sea comes up here when the tide is in,' said Julian. 'It certainly smells like it.'

The passage started getting smaller, then smaller still, until it was so low that they had to crawl along on their hands and knees. Timmy looked very funny, creeping along behind George!

Go to **300.**

'I expect he's hungry,' said Julian. 'I don't suppose the Sticks remembered to feed him before they left the island. We'd better give him something to eat and drink.'

'I'll go back to the cave and get some of Timmy's biscuits and a tin of corned beef,' said Dick. 'Shan't be long.'

He ran off, and the others sat down to wait. Jennifer settled herself quietly beside Julian, enjoying the fresh air and sunshine and the company of her rescuers.

Dick was back in no time with food and water. Tinker wolfed everything that he was given, then had a long drink. He was obviously very hungry, but as soon as he had finished his water he snapped at Timmy, then rushed back into the little room.

'Do you think we ought to take him back to the cave with us?' asked Dick. 'After all, supposing the Sticks don't come back.'

Go to **301**.

The cave was quite large, but it didn't take Julian and George long to see that Edgar wasn't there.

'Where can he have gone?' asked Julian. 'He can't possibly have come back down the passage, or we would have seen him. Either he's gone out of the front of the cave, or there's another way out of it.'

George was exploring behind a pile of rocks.

Go to **303**.

If you've arrived from **289**, *score* ◁.
If you've arrived from **307**, *score* ◁ ◁ ◁.
If you've arrived from **299**, *score* ◁ ◁ ◁ ◁.

'Right, Edgar,' said Julian. 'Stand still and don't try to run away again, or Timmy will deal with you.'

They all turned to look at the door. It was well and truly bolted. There was no sound from inside.

'Hello, there!' Julian shouted. 'Are you all right? We've come to rescue you.'

There was a scrambling noise, as if someone had got up from a stool. Then a small voice sounded from the cave.

'Hello! Who are you? Oh, please rescue me! I'm so frightened!'

'Just undoing the door!' called back Julian cheerfully. 'We're all children out here, so don't be afraid.'

He shot back the bolts and flung open the door. Inside the cave, which was lit by a lantern, stood a small girl with a scared little white face and large dark eyes. Dark red hair tumbled around her cheeks, and she had evidently been crying bitterly, for her face was dirty and tear-stained.

Go to **294.**

307

'Perhaps if you could grab hold of my legs, George,' said Julian, 'then pull as hard as you can,

I could push away from the floor of the tunnel with my hands, and with any luck I'll be free!'

George took a firm grip on Julian's ankles, and he shouted: 'Right!'

She tugged as hard as she could, wriggling back down the tunnel at the same time. It was terribly difficult, because she had nothing to brace herself against as she pulled, but eventually she heard Julian shouting at her to stop. She was back in the wide part of the tunnel by now, so she stood up. A moment or two later Julian appeared, rubbing his elbows.

'There's no point in trying to catch Edgar now,' said Julian. 'He could be anywhere. We'd better go back and wait for Dick.'

They made their way back through the maze of tunnels to the dungeon with the wooden door.

It wasn't very long before Dick appeared, dragging a sulky Edgar with him.

'Well done, Dick! He got away from us, the little horror,' said Julian.

George put Timmy to stand guard over Edgar.

Go to **306.**

308

'I think we should investigate,' said George. 'I suppose it's unlikely to be a trespasser, but we'd better have a look.'

She walked over to the doorway and glanced around the room. In one corner crouched Tinker, the Stick's hairy little dog. He was whining pitifully.

'What's the matter, Tinker?' asked George. 'Have you hurt yourself? Come here and let me have a look at you.'

She talked quietly to Tinker for a while, and eventually he walked up to her. George didn't like Tinker very much, but she hated the thought of any animal being in pain.

She picked him up and had a good look at him. For once Tinker made no effort to bite, but let George examine him.

'There doesn't seem to be anything wrong with him,' she said at last. 'I wonder why he's so miserable?'

Go to **304.**

309

It was not long before they were pulling the boat up on to the beach near Kirrin Cottage. They went straight to the police station with Jenny and told their story to a bemused constable. He sent for the inspector, who telephoned Jenny's parents.

Then the five of them and Jenny went back to Kirrin Cottage. Uncle Quentin had returned and was annoyed to find the cottage deserted. However, his anger turned to amazement when he heard about their adventure.

'How's Mother?' asked George anxiously.

'Much better,' said Uncle Quentin. 'She should be home in a couple of days.'

Soon they were joined by Mr and Mrs Armstrong, Jenny's parents, who were overjoyed at seeing their daughter safe and well. Meanwhile, the police rowed out to the island and arrested the Sticks, who had gone back there to find Edgar.

'Oh, good!' exclaimed Dick, when he heard that the Sticks were safely behind bars. 'We won't be troubled with *them* any more!'

'No,' agreed George. 'And, best of all, we can have Kirrin Island to ourselves again!'

Will the Famous Five have more adventures together?

Yes, of course they will. And perhaps YOU will be there again, too.

How many red herrings have you collected?

0–25	Very good indeed! The Famous Five must have been glad to have you with them.
26–50	Promising. Perhaps your next adventure with The Famous Five will be even more successful.
51–75	You took a long time getting there, didn't you? You'll have to do better than that to keep up with The Famous Five!
More than 75	Oh dear! Perhaps you should go back to the beginning of the story and try again.

Join the Famous Five on more of their exciting adventures in *The Famous Five and You*.